STUDIES IN GERMAN LITERATURE, LINGUISTICS, AND CULTURE
Vol. 69

STUDIES IN GERMAN LITERATURE, LINGUISTICS, AND CULTURE

Editorial Board

Frank Banta, Donald Daviau, Ingeborg Glier, Michael Hamburger,
Gerhart Hoffmeister, Herbert Knust, Wulf Koepke, Victor Lange,
James Lyon, Michael Metzger, Hans-Gert Roloff, John Spalek,
Eitel Timm, Frank Trommler, Heinz Wetzel

Managing Editors

James Hardin and Gunther Holst
(South Carolina)

CAMDEN HOUSE
Columbia, South Carolina

Robert H. Brown

Nature's Hidden Terror

VIOLENT NATURE IMAGERY IN EIGHTEENTH-CENTURY GERMANY

CAMDEN HOUSE

Copyright © 1991 by
CAMDEN HOUSE, INC.

Published by Camden House, Inc.
Drawer 2025
Columbia, SC 29202 USA

Set in Garamond type and printed on acid-free paper.
Binding materials are chosen for strength and
durability.

All Rights Reserved
Printed in the United States of America
First Edition

Library of Congress Cataloging-in-Publication Data

Brown, Robert H., 1952-
 Nature's hidden terror : violent nature imagery in eighteenth
-century Germany / Robert H. Brown. -- 1st ed.
  p.   cm. -- (Studies in German literature, linguistics, and
culture ; vol. 69)
 Based on the author's dissertation.
 Includes bibliographical references and index.
 ISBN 1-879751-06-2
 1. German literature--18th century--History and criticism.
2. Nature in literature. 3. Violence in literature. 4. Social
change in literature. I. Title. II. Series: Studies in German
literature, linguistics, and culture ; v. 69.
PT289.B68 1991
830.9'355--dc20   91-22164
                                                          CIP

Contents

1	Nature Imagery and Social Change	1
2	The Lisbon Earthquake	23
3	Nature and Family in Gerstenberg's *Ugolino*	56
4	Nature and Self in Goethe's *Werther*	73
5	Nature and History in Schiller's *Räuber*	108
6	Nature's Hidden Terror	130
	Works Consulted	138
	Index	147

Acknowledgments

I would like to thank Professor Hinrich C. Seeba for his support in directing the dissertation on which this study is based. Thanks also to Professors Martin E. Jay and Frederic C. Tubach for their critical comments. Special thanks are due to Sigrid Brauner, Edda Brunner, and Carlos Velasquez for their criticisms and proofreading, and to Wendi Goodwin for word-processing help. I deeply appreciate the patience and support over the years of my friend Margaret Miner and my parents, Robert C. and Joan T. Brown. Finally, thanks to Professor James Hardin for his expert help in revising the manuscript for publication.

RHB
June 1991

Preface

THIS STUDY GREW OUT of my fascination with violent nature imagery in eighteenth-century Germany: the earthquakes, floods, storms, and similar phenomena that increasingly found their way into German literature. Why, at a time of social upheaval across Europe, was there a growing literary interest in violent nature? Is there a connection?

This question presumes twofold: that social history can be meaningfully reconstructed; and that literature sheds light on it. The first assumption may seem questionable. Since history invariably reflects the historian's bias, it is impossible to reconstruct what really happened. The problem with this objection is its impracticality. Since present-day choices are informed by the past, there is no alternative to reconstructing history. Of course, any history is colored by the historian's interest, which must be made clear: my interest is in exploring attitudes toward social change in eighteenth-century Germany.

My second assumption is that literature is a historical document. Unlike other such documents, literature offers insight not into what happened, but into how what was happening was perceived. In reflecting on contemporary conflict, literature shapes cultural attitudes toward change, a process with profound implications. Troubling German responses to modern change in the twentieth century may find echoes in much earlier texts.

This consideration motivates my study. Germany in the eighteenth century saw the ascendancy of state-subsidized social sectors with ill-defined roles in traditional society (civil servants, entrepreneurs, and professionals). These sectors used literature to express their doubts and aspirations in a changing world. Nature imagery was well-suited to this purpose: on the one hand, it projected permanence and originality, or the preservation of tradition; on the other, it offered new horizons for exploring alternative identities. The central question is this: were the alternatives found in nature full of hope for the future, or did they express an underlying fear of modern change?

Since my method relies on close readings, I include many quotations. The original German has been included in footnotes. All translations from the German are my own. The single texts I work with in Chapters Three through Five are documented only once. The footnoted original is followed by an indication of where it can be found in the text. My hope is to present a fresh perspective on eighteenth-century German literature.

1

Nature Imagery and Social Change

ON OCTOBER 17, 1989, an earthquake measured at 7.1 on the Richter scale rocked the San Francisco Bay Area. Dozens perished under collapsing buildings and freeways. Following the disaster, a letter appeared in a local newspaper warning of "the hand of an angry God in this disaster."

> This was no "accident." We know from the Bible that God chastises His children when they go astray. Abortion, homosexuality, immodesty and the like, shall never be tolerated by the eternal Father in Heaven. This quake is just a warning. It is a call to repentance. Should the abominations continue, we should expect more frequent and more intense earthquakes.[1]

It had been over two centuries since the Portuguese Jesuit Gabriel Malagrida similarly importuned his countrymen following the Lisbon earthquake disaster of 1755. Malagrida was executed, his notions ridiculed in Voltaire's *Candide* (1759). Nevertheless, the belief persists that nature is divinely imbued with moral imperatives, the violation of which produces earthquakes. How has an anachronism discredited over 200 years ago endured?

This question goes to the heart of a matter that has long puzzled scholars: why has myth thrived side by side with faith in scientific reason? Although the claim of scientific reason to universal truth was well established by the late eighteenth century, violent nature imagery still flourished. What configuration did it assume? What role did it play in the

---

[1] *San Francisco Chronicle*, 25 October 1989, editorial page.

changes that were transforming Germany from a traditional into a modern society? This study explores these questions in an effort to locate the continuing appeal of nature imagery despite the demystification of nature by the Enlightenment.

The letter calling on San Franciscans to turn to God following the 1989 earthquake draws on a central tradition of Western nature mythology contained in the Bible. In *Genesis*, nature is both a heavenly Garden of Eden and an earthly wasteland from which humanity must wrest a toilsome living. In disobeying God by partaking of the Tree of Knowledge, Adam transforms the former into the latter. Originally good, nature becomes difficult and dangerous when corrupted by sin. The prophet who warns San Francisco of further earthquakes appeals to the Biblical myth of nature corrupted by sin when he attributes violent nature to divine punishment.

Implicit in the story of the Fall is a dualistic vision of nature itself: on the one hand, nature is an ideal world of harmony and wholeness from which man, when he enters society (the archetypal family formed with Eve), departs and towards which he subsequently strives (paradise); on the other hand, nature is the fallen or depraved, sinful world of empirical reality in which man must earn his bread by the sweat of his brow. This dualistic vision of nature informs Christianity.

Antiquity similarly attributes nature's violence to its corruption by human depravity. The ancient vision of a *locus amoenus* projects ideals of balance and harmony onto nature itself, while Phaeton's overweening pride in steering Apollo's chariot scorches the earth and kills him. In Biblical and Greek mythology, nature's beneficence or malevolence reflects human ideals and human misbehavior. Those who fail to abide by certain codes of behavior are punished by natural disasters, which are sure signs of transgression.

The power of the nature myth is predicated on the entrenched belief that nature is inherently good, that nature and society are antithetical, that society ("culture," "civilization") corrupts nature, and that nature responds with destructive violence. Hayden White has called the ancient view of a pristine nature corrupted by society "quintessentially a radical doctrine." "For basic to it," he declares, "is the conviction that men are really the same throughout all time and space but have been made evil in certain times and places by the imposition of social restraints upon them."[2] The belief in a nature uncorrupted by the evils of civilization implicitly criticizes those evils while envisioning a better, more "natural"

---

[2] Hayden White, *Tropics of Discourse* (Baltimore: Johns Hopkins Press, 1978), 171.

social order. Raymond Williams cites many instances in antiquity of idyllic nature imagery used as social critique.[3]

However, the connotations of primitive nature as an antitype to a corrupt society are not always radical. The prophet who warns San Francisco against the "abominations" of "abortion, homosexuality, immodesty and the like" condemns the freedom of others to choose alternative lifestyles. Modern advertising often uses the belief in the inherent superiority of nature to civilization in order to manipulate consumption in ways that have little to do with emancipation or social criticism. The "Blut und Boden" ideology of German fascism justified racism in the name of "the realm of the organic," legitimating murder by appealing to the natural origins of race and nation and their corruption by Western civilization. The mythology of nature has been used in ways that are affirmative rather than subversive, and repressive rather than emancipatory.

In fact, the nature myth seems wide open to ready manipulative use. Whether invoked by religious prophets or social critics, its components remain the same. Each age or group interprets them according to its own interests and needs.

What is the origin of the ancient belief in nature's inherent superiority? In *Work on Myth* (1979), Hans Blumenberg situates all myth at the beginnings of human evolution. When man descended from the trees to the savannah, he had to stand upright to find food and see enemies. The "absolute reality" of confrontation with a suddenly hostile environment produced myth, Blumenberg argues, because it provided ways of dealing with the new environment. In a process of selection over millennia of story-telling, the myths that most effectively suited this purpose survived.[4]

Blumenberg's theory reproduces the myth it seeks to explain: it posits an original antithesis between man and nature. The relative suddenness in geological terms of human appearance in the savannah does not exclude a gradual process of evolution. The first bands of humans may have acclimated to slowly changing surroundings as forest gave way to savannah, never encountering an environment more hostile at any one time than at any other.

Moreover, an original confrontation with a hostile savannah does not explain myth's persistence once the new environment was tamed. The notion of an "absolute reality" makes sense only as a metaphor for a

---

[3] Raymond Williams, *The Country and the City* (New York: Oxford UP, 1973).

[4] Hans Blumenberg, *Work on Myth*, trans. Robert M. Wallace (Cambridge and London: MIT Press, 1985).

continuing process of confronting a perpetually changing environment. Whether the anxiety produced under the pressure of social and environmental change engenders mythical explanations begs the point: it does not explain why scientific explanations have not displaced mythical ones.

Less obscure than myth's origins are the ways in which it reflects the values of certain ages and groups. When Blumenberg apposes man to a hostile savannah, he projects the image of a solitary individual or band in confrontation not only with nature, but also with other humans in the savannah. This image of an isolated individual or group in confrontation with a hostile natural and social environment is typical of a particular stage in what Norbert Elias calls the civilizing process: the modern era of defining reality in terms of individual experience.[5] Blumenberg uses a key component of the nature myth — the antagonism between nature and society — to posit what Elias calls the "homo clausus," the isolated individual out of touch with others and in constant struggle with them for domination. The myth of nature is used to propagate modern values of individualism and competition.

Violent nature imagery was not always used to profile the isolated individual. In his essay "The Forms of Wildness," Hayden White explores the myth of wilderness and "its traditional occupant, the Wild Man" in Western culture.[6] According to White, the traditional Wild Man is not a refugee from civilization (the intrepid Crusoe-like figure or noble savage of eighteenth-century literature still recognizable in Blumenberg's ape-man), but a terrifying barbarian — the human embodiment of nature's menace. "In the Christian Middle Ages," White notes, "...the Wild Man is the distillation of the specific anxieties underlying the three securities supposedly provided by the specifically Christian institutions of civilized life," including the sustenance afforded by the political, social, and economic institutions of feudalism.[7] As savage foil to feudal civilization, the Wild Man served to illustrate its advantages while threatening those who would challenge the security of its confines.

Seventeenth-century emblematic allegory offers similar instances of violent nature imagery used to buttress the social status quo. In depicting a ship running to harbor before a storm ("Mein oft bestürmtes Schiff" — 1639), Andreas Gryphius discusses the salvation of the soul in fleeing worldly temptation and embracing the Church, or on another

---

[5] Norbert Elias, *The History of Manners*, Volume 1 of *The Civilizing Process*, trans. Edmund Jephcott (New York: Pantheon Books, 1978).

[6] White, 154.

[7] White, 166.

level the security that lies in death and the afterlife following this vale of tears. Nature in the form of Gryphius's storm allegorizes both worldly sin and the process of seeking and finding salvation in the harbor. On one level, the storm serves to excoriate impious behavior by distancing it from the harbor of the Church; on another level, the storm appears part of a higher natural order, God's emblematic hand-writing pointing to salvation. Gryphius uses the image of nature's violence to ward off threats to a God-centered hierarchy while propagating that hierarchy as part of a higher natural order.

In the eighteenth century, violent nature changed from an emblem of God's eternal order into the symbol of a changing world. Reviving the ancient tradition of nature imagery as social commentary, the eighteenth century developed nature into what Robert Spaemann calls a "concept of emancipation," whether conceived by Dietrich Freiherr von Holbach and Jean-Jacques Rousseau as the "liberation of nature" from a "history of repression," or by Immanuel Kant, Friedrich Schiller, and others as the "liberation from nature" of "reason" within the history of nature itself.[8] Nature became a rallying cry to political agendas (for instance, the appeal to natural rights) and a polemical tool against opposing persuasions. After 1789, violent nature was often used as a metaphor for revolution by sympathizers and critics alike.[9] In the eighteenth century, the appeal to nature and the use of nature imagery became ways for all sides to react to contemporary developments while exploring or judging their outcomes.

Nature's Fear and Fascination

Götz Großklaus has developed a systematic analysis of eighteenth-century nature imagery. He points out a dialectic inherent in the modern aesthetic exploration of wild nature, which opens up unfamiliar terrain (*Entgrenzung*) while simultaneously delimiting and dominating newly explored terrain (*Eingrenzung*) in a way that locks out and pro-

---

[8] Robert Spaemann, "Genetisches zum Naturbegriff des 18. Jahrhunderts," in *Archiv für Begriffsgeschichte* 11 (1967), 60-61.

[9] Hans-Wolf Jäger documents the use of winter, spring, floods, melting ice, the wolf, the lion, storms, the sea, streams, rocks, cliffs, and dams to symbolize political struggle in the period 1789-1848. Hans-Wolf Jäger, "Das Naturbild als politische Metapher im Vormärz," in *Zur Literatur der Restaurationsepoche*, ed. Jost Hermand and Manfred Windfuhr (Stuttgart: Metzler, 1970), 405-440.

tects from as yet unexplored and unconquered nature spaces.[10] He draws a correlation between periods of aesthetic exploration of nature and eras of social and political upheaval (such as 1750-1840 or 1880-1930), and he hypothesizes a literary role in testing the waters of social and political change and thereby spearheading it.

For instance, Großklaus notes a growing aesthetic interest in Alpine scenery in the early eighteenth century (such as Albrecht Haller's influential ode *Die Alpen* in 1729). Before, mountainous terrain was deemed frightening and therefore hidden from travelers' view by coach curtains or opaque glass.[11] According to Großklaus, the desire to cross into unfamiliar (Alpine) nature terrain at once represented and cultivated a broader desire to cross borders and overcome traditional social and cultural barriers. Exploring nature paved the way for exploring new social possibilities. The longing for the unfamiliarity of unexplored nature implied dissatisfaction with the old corporative order (*Ständegesellschaft*) and its absolutist state. Traditionally, the old order was represented in nature as a rationally structured hierarchy, a closed system reaching from lowly "myriads in the peopled grass" (as Alexander Pope puts it in his *Essay on Man* — 1736) to God. The discovery of unfamiliar horizons in nature broke open this symbolic structure, Großklaus argues, threatening its hegemony. "Long before the political revolutions of 1789 and 1848," he maintains, "certain revolutions of the prevalent symbolic structure are to be assumed."[12]

The eighteenth-century desire to explore the unexplored in nature was coupled with a yen for heights. The new fascination with the Alps and other mountain ranges was partly due to the solitude they provided the individual traveller, who could enjoy what Großklaus calls a "dominating perspective" (*Herrscherblick*) from once-feared mountain peaks. Self-discovery in nature not only challenged traditional codes of perception, it established new ones oriented toward the hegemony of the isolated individual over his environment.

---

[10] Götz Großklaus, "Der Naturtraum des Kulturbürgers," in *Natur als Gegenwelt*, ed. Götz Großklaus and Ernst Oldemeyer (Karlsruhe: von Loeper, 1983), 169-196; Großklaus, "Reisen in die fremde Natur - Zur Fremdenwahrnehmung im Kontext der bürgerlichen Aufstiegsgeschichte," in Großklaus and Oldemeyer, 265-276.

[11] D. G. Charlton discusses this phenomenon in *New Images of the Natural in France* (Cambridge: Cambridge UP, 1984), 42-43.

[12] "Weit im Vorfeld der politischen Revolutionen von 1789 und 1848 wären bestimmte Umwälzungen der sinngebenden symbolischen Struktur anzunehmen." Großklaus, "Naturtraum," 182.

As Großklaus notes, however, the panoramic vistas described by eighteenth-century Alpine travellers typically reflect awe tinged with fear. On one evening in 1779, Johann Wolfgang Goethe compared advancing shadows on ice-covered mountains near Montblanc to the way "an enormous body expires from outward toward the heart." This apparition of enormity and death in nature "appeared almost frightening."[13] Before, in the same account, Goethe describes how "the whole Pays de Vaud and de Gex lay like a map beneath us, all properties cut off with green fences.... Villages, towns, country houses and ... chalets ... shone toward the sun." In this view of nature spaces enclosed and bordered by fences and settlements, there is no hint of fearfulness, only an indescribable "grandeur and beauty of this sight."[14]

In the eighteenth century, titillating encounters with danger in nature were considered sublime.[15] The word "sublime" derives from Latin words meaning "under the door."[16] A sublime experience slips past borders and barriers to confront life itself in unadulterated form, which may prove frightening. By way of compensation, something familiar tends to be projected into the foreground of a sublime view (such as Goethe's bordered spaces) in order to protect from nature's menacing reaches.

The framing-and-taming technique of dealing with nature's menace led, according to Großklaus, to nature's colonization. "It is this [eighteenth-century] avant-garde," Großklaus observes, "that uses a nature still alien, wild and untamed ... to practice that colonization of Alpine nature space" experienced today as sight-seeing, skiing, and other forms

---

[13] "...wie ein gewaltiger Körper von außen gegen das Herz zu abstirbt.... [Es] sah fast ängstlich aus." Johann Wolfgang Goethe, *Goethe-Gedenkausgabe: Biographische Einzelschriften* (Zurich: Artemis, 1949), IX, 20, quoted in Großklaus, "Naturtraum," 187.

[14] "...das ganze Pays de Vaud und de Gex lag wie eine Flurkarte unter uns, alle Besitzungen mit grünen Zäunen abgeschnitten.... Dörfer, Städtchen, Landhäuser und ... Sennhütten ... leuchteten gegen die Sonne." What impressed Goethe was "das Große und Schöne dieses Anblicks." Goethe, *Gedenkausgabe*, 18-19, quoted in Großklaus, "Naturtraum," 186-187.

[15] "Whatever is fitted in any sort to excite the ideas of pain, and danger...," Edmund Burke wrote in 1755, "is a source of the sublime." Edmund Burke, *A Philosophical Enquiry into the Origin of our Ideas about the Sublime and Beautiful* (London: Routledge & Kegan Paul, 1958), 39, quoted in Charlton, 44.

[16] See Joseph T. Shipley, *Dictionary of Word Origins* (New York: Philosophical Library, 1945), 215.

of tourism and recreation.[17] For Großklaus, a fascination with untamed nature leads to its exploration, while fear of it motivates its transformation into objects useful in bourgeois culture and society. A dialectic of fear and fascination characterizes the modern exploration of new horizons in nature, which eliminates the threat of the unfamiliar by exploiting newly conquered terrain.

While German cultural contributions to nature's exploitation are well worth studying, the fearful side of nature imagery poses another question as well, one that Großklaus does not raise: if eighteenth-century nature imagery suggests the bold exploration of new horizons, might it not also suggest a fearful retreat from them? Großklaus focuses on eighteenth-century writers as apostles of modernity who eagerly explored nature in order to exploit it. From this point of view, both fear of and fascination with wild nature embrace processes of change: in entering the fascinating terrain of wild nature, eighteenth-century writers expanded the cultural horizons of possibility, paving the way for social transformation; and in banishing nature's hidden terrors by colonizing nature, the same writers prepared the way for nature's exploitation on an unprecedented scale.

Both processes coincided with the subsumption of nature and society under the individual. The young German authors of the late eighteenth century reveled in a cult of personality. Their articulation of spontaneity, individuality, feeling, and originality challenged a traditional order based on authority by birthright and knowing one's place. Their nature imagery replaced traditional symbolic codes with personal subjectivity and the hegemony of the individual over his environment.

However, the eighteenth-century imagination of nature's fearful side may have embraced contemporary change on one level while recoiling from it on another. Negative portrayals of social or political change using violent nature metaphors flourished after the French Revolution (for instance, in Goethe's poem "Der Zauberlehrling" in 1797), and they are commonly attributed to political backlash in Germany against the Revolution. But dark or violent nature imagery infused many pre-Revolutionary works as well, particularly in the period framed by the Lisbon earthquake of 1755 and the events of 1789. If this period, too, expressed unease about contemporary change, then the French Revolution may have been less of a turning point in German cultural history than some-

---

[17] "Es ist diese Avantgarde [seit der Mitte des 18. Jahrhunderts] die gewissermaßen am Objekt der noch fremden, wilden und unbefriedeten Natur ... jene Kolonisierung des Natur-Raums der Alpen [einübt]." Großklaus, "Naturtraum," 179.

times thought.[18] A fascination with what Goethe called demonic nature may reflect a budding fear of modernity with fateful implications for nineteenth- and twentieth-century German history.

The purpose of this study is to raise the question of whether eighteenth-century German writings before 1789 demonstrate not only an eagerness to explore new horizons, but also a deep-seated fear of them. While German conservatism as a coherent ideological response to social and political change has been traced to the writings of Justus Möser,[19] his literary contemporaries in the Sturm und Drang are widely believed to have radicalized the Enlightenment's demands for social change. I have chosen to examine Gerstenberg's *Ugolino* (1767), Goethe's *Die Leiden des jungen Werther* (1774), and Schiller's *Die Räuber* (1781), partly because they frame the "radical" Sturm und Drang period. All three works develop a rebellious cult of personality, and all feature dark or violent nature imagery such as storms, floods, and deep forests. If the fearsome nature imagery in these works can be linked to a fear of contemporary social change, then it might be argued that they articulated a conservative reaction to the prospect of social and political change in Germany well before the French Revolution.

All three works treat a common problem central to the imagination of contemporary audiences: the isolation and endangerment of the individual on the periphery of traditional society. In each work, the protagonists are situated outside of traditional society, whether by force or by choice. This isolation is expressed as an apposition between society and nature, which is projected in each work as an "other" terrain of both hope and fear. Each work features the problem of identity and the experience of self in nature, and each presents a vision of what it could mean to live unbound by traditional fetters and governed instead by non-traditional values of individualism, egoism, and the marketplace.

Is this vision of social change promising or horrifying? Does nature ultimately turn on those it seduces in a paroxysm of violence that destroys them? The answer to this question informs what I consider to be

---

[18] According to one literary history, "Die relative Einheitlichkeit der Literaturperiode von Gottsched bis zu den Stürmern und Drängern, die in der aufklärerischen Funktionsbestimmung der Literatur begründet war, ging in der Auseinandersetzung mit der französischen Revolution verloren." Wolfgang Beutin et al, *Deutsche Literaturgeschichte* (Stuttgart: Metzler, 1979), 133. Implicit here is the assumption that the whole period 1740-1789 was uniform in its progressive literary message, and that the French Revolution changed this.

[19] Klaus Epstein, *The Genesis of German Conservatism* (Princeton, NJ: Princeton UP, 1966), 297-338.

the subtext of each work: a discourse on the changes that were transforming Germany from a traditional to a modern society. Do these changes unleash demonic forces of destruction in nature signifying revulsion toward modern change? Or does change lead in a positive, constructive direction full of hope for the future? The answers to these questions bear upon the formation of German cultural attitudes towards social and political change with implications even today.

Modern Change

These questions assume that modern change was already underway in eighteenth-century Germany. By modernity, I mean what Walter Lepenies calls the age of transition toward the industrialization of Europe on a large scale from about 1750 to 1900.[20] Of course, German industrialization was largely delayed until the nineteenth century, and parts of Germany remained pre-modern into the twentieth century. Nevertheless, the social, economic, and political formations associated with industrialization were already developing long before 1800, indicating the direction in which Germany was moving. Their description below is intended to show the context of historical change in which eighteenth-century literature was embedded.

The period from 1600 to 1750 in Europe was characterized by stagnating or declining populations, trade, industry, and prices, particularly in southern and central Europe.[21] "It affected countries unequally," notes economic historian Jan De Vries, "some never recovered while others were set back only briefly and even gained competitive advantages."[22] Germany, too, was unevenly affected by the crisis, which was especially hard in the south and east. In part, this was due to the Thirty Years' War, although its effects should not be exaggerated. "Aside from the fact that the timing of military destruction and economic stagnation does not lend unqualified support to this view," De Vries observes, "the major weakness of the argument is that the destruction and dislocation of warfare was local and that a compensating economic stimulus of

---

[20] Walter Lepenies, "Die Dynamisierung des Naturbegriffs an der Wende zur Neuzeit," in *Das Naturbild des Menschen*, ed. Jörg Zimmermann (Munich: Fink, 1982), 285.

[21] Jan De Vries, *The Economy of Europe in an Age of Crisis* (London: Cambridge UP, 1976), 1-29.

[22] De Vries, 21.

orders for equipment and payments for services very likely made up for these losses."[23]

De Vries argues that during this period of apparent decline, the foundations were laid for the subsequent industrial boom period in Europe from 1750 to 1900. De Vries diverges from the established wisdom that primitive capital was accumulated through trade expansion and the exploitation of colonies. Instead, he perceives social and economic forces at work that from 1600 to 1750 freed up resources held in check by traditional agrarian economies in Europe itself. The logic of absolutism stimulated the growth of regional markets, transferring labor and resources from traditional to modern modes of production. This explanation for primitive capital accumulation is particularly attractive for Germany, which never had significant colonies to exploit. Even if the capital accumulation that De Vries describes for the Atlantic seaboard was largely delayed in Germany until after 1800, the social and political dynamic that led territorial governments to pursue policies that favored capital formation was established well before then.[24]

Particularly in Prussia, the driving force behind this dynamic was the emergence of a sovereign territorial state. As Geoffrey Barraclough notes, the Treaty of Westphalia (1648) destroyed the last vestiges of imperial authority.[25] The various German states were left to compete with one another and with surrounding European powers for what the emerging doctrine of mercantilism defined as the source of wealth and power: populated territories. "A fundamental rule of governments," remarked Frederick II of Prussia, "is the principle of extending their territories."[26] For the states that emerged from the Thirty Years' War, survival depended on a combination of diplomacy and military power. "In the final reckoning," Isser Woloch points out, "a state's interests could be assured only by overwhelming strength. More than skillful

---

[23] De Vries, 22.

[24] Theodore Hamerow points out that at least in Saxony and the Rhineland, large-scale industrial production dates to the eighteenth century. However, an indication that capital formation was largely delayed in Germany until after 1800 is that the number of joint stock companies rose from a scant five in 1800 to over 25 in 1825 and 100 in 1850. Theodore B. Hamerow, *Restoration, Revolution, Reaction* (Princeton, NJ: Princeton UP, 1972), 6.

[25] Geoffrey Barraclough, *The Origins of Modern Germany* (New York: W. W. Norton & Co, 1984), 388.

[26] Quoted in Isser Woloch, *Eighteenth-Century Europe* (New York: W. W. Norton & Co, 1982), 37.

diplomacy, state-building was the key to survival: armies, taxes to support the armies, and bureaucrats to collect the taxes."[27]

In the petty principalities, this state-building mobilization of resources often had an adverse effect. "Hence all liquid capital available," Barraclough observes, "when the voracious needs of princely pomp had been satisfied, was applied to building up armies and bureaucracies."[28] However, in larger territories like Prussia, the concentration of resources by the state led to a kind of court capitalism that stimulated a growing market sector. The courts borrowed from private bankers, then contracted with manufacturers and merchants to procure what they needed to equip and maintain large standing armies. This contributed to the circulation of capital and the growth of incipient capitalist enterprises in non-traditional industries with economies of scale, such as textiles and heavy metals. Through concentration of government demand, conferral of monopolies, exemption from guild regulation, and other forms of subsidy, the state stimulated incipient capitalist enterprises, leading to a growing market-oriented work force, particularly in rural areas (for instance, linen-bleaching in Wuppertal).

The burden of expanding state taxes ultimately fell on the peasants, who had to spend less time producing household necessities and more time producing for the market in order to generate the cash needed to pay taxes. Since they therefore no longer produced part or all of what they consumed, the peasants were forced to compensate by generating even more cash, and their growing market activity contributed to rising market demand. A symbiotic relationship developed between the state, military power, and the market economy, drawing growing numbers out of traditional forms of production into non-traditional ones, while simultaneously further divorcing both production and consumption from more-or-less immediate interaction with nature.

This dynamic tended to shake the foundations of traditional society as territorial governments pursued policies that undermined the very stability and continuity they were designed to preserve. "The irony remains," De Vries observes, "that policies inspired by a desire for order and stability so often acted to unbind the fetters of the local peasant economy and thereby encourage the social stratification and market orientation that was, in time, to destroy much of what absolutism had wished to preserve."[29]

---

[27] Woloch, 13.

[28] Barraclough, 390.

[29] De Vries, 244.

Social Stratification

The social stratification that tended to undermine the traditional order in the eighteenth century has been well documented.[30] Traditional society was organized into cohesive caste-like bodies, each with certain social, economic, political, intellectual, and military duties and privileges defined by custom and law. Each person's place in society was predetermined by the estate (*Stand*) he or she was born into, which in turn functioned by written or unwritten rules to preserve its own niche in the overall system.

Traditionally, the estates enjoyed a measure of autonomy from central authority articulated in the feudal diets. The political history of the German Middle Ages is marked by the attempts of each estate to defend or expand its rights and privileges at the expense of others. Since the estates (or corporative entities) formed the system's central units, it has been dubbed "corporative society" (*Ständegesellschaft*).

In the eighteenth century, state policies encouraged the growth of social sectors that did not belong to the traditional estates. Active on the marketplace, these sectors competed with the corporative system for resources and members. Despite their rapid growth in the eighteenth century, however, these new social sectors were outside of what remained a corporative mainstream, particularly in what Mack Walker calls "German Home Towns," small and medium-size cities (like Justus Möser's Osnabrück) where traditionalism persisted into the twentieth century.[31]

The rise of standing armies after the Thirty Years' War created a large new social sector — Prussia's army alone expanded from 6,000 in 1660 to 200,000 in 1786.[32] Government spending in support of the court and bureaucracy as well as in paying pensions, subsidies, and interest on government bonds raised the number of retainers, pensioners, and those who lived from investments as well as the number of servants they depended on. State policies also stimulated the growth of an industrial work force.

---

[30] Besides Woloch, see Henri Brunschwig, *Enlightenment and Romanticism in Eighteenth-Century Prussia* (Chicago, London: University of Chicago Press, 1974), 101-146, and W. H. Bruford, *Germany in the Eighteenth Century* (Cambridge: Cambridge UP, 1968), 131-269.

[31] Mack Walker, *German Home Towns* (Ithaca: Cornell UP, 1971).

[32] Woloch, 52. If about a third of Prussia's five million inhabitants in 1786 were economically active, then about one in ten was a soldier.

The most dynamic of the new social sectors included a new breed of entrepreneurs and civil servants with close ties to the territorial state. This sector incorporated merchants and industrialists who, as De Vries puts it, "exploited the new opportunities created by growing government demand, an increasingly efficient commercial network connecting the Atlantic ports, and the cost-reducing potential of rural industry."[33] The new businesses and especially the state that subsidized them required an army of educated administrators; a way out of prospective poverty for many in the traditional bourgeoisie and aristocracy was to study for the civil service.

Jürgen Habermas mentions a third group affiliated with the state: the academics, teachers, lawyers, doctors, clergymen, and other professionals who were beholden to the state's academies and institutions for their education and often for their livelihood.[34] The state-sponsored entrepreneurs, bureaucrats, and professionals together formed what Rolf Grimminger calls a "new elite of the economy and the mind," precipitating "a global change in traditional corporative society."[35] While the old estates continued to dominate society, a new, highly mobile sector emerged on the fringes. Its hegemony over local bureaucracy, the state-supported economy, and the literary market tended to subvert traditional corporative hierarchies.

The rising demand for soldiers, domestics, rural workers, and civil servants in the eighteenth century was more than offset by a population surge due to stabilizing food supplies. Hoping to build the tax base, the territorial governments encouraged agricultural innovation (such as the introduction of the potato) and sponsored projects designed to expand food production (including Frederick II's efforts to open new agricultural land in the east). As the population mushroomed, growing competition for the restricted number of spaces available within the corporative system of guilds and semi-feudal peasant holdings raised the number of vagrants, beggars, thieves, bandits, smugglers, and extortionists. While this sector was neither new nor particularly market-oriented, its growth suggests the inability of traditional corporative structures to meet the challenge of state-sponsored economic change.

---

[33] De Vries, 234-235.

[34] Jürgen Habermas, *Strukturwandel der Öffentlichkeit*, (Neuwied: Luchterhand, 1965), 37.

[35] A "neue Elite der Wirtschaft und des Geistes" caused "einen globalen Wandel der altständischen Gesellschaft." Rolf Grimminger, "Aufklärung, Absolutismus und bürgerliche Individuen," *Hansers Sozialgeschichte der Literatur* (Munich: Hanser, 1980), III, 88.

Although traditional life continued unaltered for the vast majority of Germans, state policy nonetheless stimulated the unprecedented growth of social sectors on the fringes of traditional corporative society. Various in character and origin, and spanning the spectrum from rags to riches, the rural workers and their employers, the petty farmers and farm laborers, the domestic and civil servants, and the rest of the modern social sectors had little in common beyond displacement from traditional corporative society. Since this was their salient feature in the overall corporative context of eighteenth-century society, they may be described as "non-corporative."

From a literary standpoint, the most important of the non-corporative strata was what Grimminger calls the new bourgeoisie: the state-supported businessmen, civil servants, and professionals.[36] The sobriquet "new" serves to distinguish these elements from their traditional bourgeois counterparts in the towns. The urban patricians and guild masters enjoyed representation in the territorial diets of the estates and were often at odds with the territorial state, which was bent on undermining their control of the towns. By contrast, the new bourgeoisie participated in the state or was subsidized by it. While the traditional bourgeoisie was rooted in the old order, the new bourgeoisie was both divorced from it and involved in subverting it through the state.

However, the new bourgeoisie is not to be confused with the stereotypical capitalists of the nineteenth century. Much of it came from traditional sectors in the cities or countryside and still shared traditional values. Still, it formed the nucleus of the modern capitalist class that would dominate Germany in the next century. In particular, the tendency of its entrepreneurial element to accumulate capital was already pronounced, and since the state both depended on and supported this element, a modern capitalist market orientation and a corresponding ethic of individualism tended to infuse the state bureaucracy.

The new bourgeoisie differed sharply in status, education, and prosperity from the popular sectors that comprised the bulk of the non-corporative strata: the servants, workers, soldiers, market-oriented peasants, and unemployed. Yet it was not identical with the state. Although dependent on the state, the new bourgeoisie articulated its own particular interests, which gradually diverged from those of Germany's powerful princes. It was isolated not only from the traditional estates,

---

[36] Grimminger uses the term *die neuen Bürgerlichen*. Grimminger, 88. While he does not include professionals in this sector, their ties to the state, though perhaps more indirect, would seem to place them in it.

but also from non-corporative ruling and working strata above and below.

The principal forum of the new bourgeoisie was on the literary market. According to Arnold Hauser, eighteenth-century literature "turned bourgeois" in three key ways: a new reading public included the prosperous bourgeoisie and middle classes; writers grew more independent and self-confident; and a literary marketplace developed as publishing houses began to supplement or even supplant the patronage system.[37] By the late eighteenth century, literature — in the broad sense of published texts — was written principally for a market dominated by a new sector of professionals, civil servants, and entrepreneurs relatively unencumbered by traditional corporative ties, and bound in one way or another not to the person of the prince, but to the state.

Through what Habermas calls "the medium of public reason," the new bourgeoisie used literature (especially the periodicals) to advance its own interests against the state. The reading public appropriated the state-regulated public sphere in order to come to terms with the state on the rules that governed the "privatized but publicly relevant sphere of production."[38] However, the state was not always pleased with what the new bourgeoisie had to say. Through censorship and punishment, the state set parameters of acceptable public discourse designed to promote its own political interests. As early as 1758, Gotthold Ephraim Lessing wrote to J. W. L. Gleim that "on pain of great punishment, not a single line may be printed in Berlin without censorship and permission."[39] By the late eighteenth century, the new bourgeoisie found itself on a collision course with the most powerful political actor on the contemporary stage: the territorial state.

The Politics of Isolation

---

[37] Arnold Hauser, *Sozialgeschichte der Kunst und Literatur* (Munich: Beck, 1953), 513-750.

[38] "...privatisierte aber öffentlich relevante Produktionssphäre." Habermas, 42.

[39] "...bei großer Strafe, nicht eine Zeile ohne Zensur und Erlaubnis hier in Berlin gedruckt werden darf." Letter of 16 December 1758 to Gleim. According to Habermas, there was censorship in Halle as early as 1729; Christian Friedrich Schubart, who first published *Deutsche Chronik* in 1774, was sentenced to ten years in prison for its improprieties, and Wilhelm Ludwig Wekhrlin, who began editing *Felleisen* in 1778, died in prison for doing so. Habermas, 35, 94.

The role of the territorial state, like that of its imperial predecessor, was to defend territorial borders while preserving the corporative order from within. With the rise of absolutism, these two mandates of territorial government came into conflict. The traditional prerogatives of the estates, which implied a weak central government, became a hindrance to territorial defense. The same centrifugal forces that rendered the German Empire prone to foreign depredations threatened the sovereign territories themselves. If they remained weak confederations of estates, they were threatened by outside powers. In Sweden or Poland, where the estates jealously guarded their privileges and kept central authority weak, the state either declined or disappeared in the eighteenth century, its territory swallowed by powerful neighbors.[40] In order to survive, the state had to mobilize territorial resources in its defense, and for this it needed to win control of them from the estates.

Between 1519 and 1750, Germany's territorial princes whittled away corporative privileges. They took advantage of the religious schism to bind both Protestant and Catholic Churches to secular authority, the support of which both the Reformation and Counter Reformation needed in order to prevail. By 1648, the churches were among what Barraclough calls "the most solid supports" of princely sovereignty.[41]

With the clergy tamed, the princes "sought to drive home their advantage by attacking the nobility and the towns and freeing themselves from dependence on the States-General [*Landtage*]," according to Barraclough.[42] They used their own burgeoning administrative machinery to supplant the autonomous regimes of the towns and regional overlords and to end the estates' participation in taxation. "Taxation and legislation," Barraclough notes, "became prerogatives of the ruler, and supported by a bureaucratic system ... and by a mercenary army, the princes emerged from the ruin of the Thirty Years' War as absolute rulers."[43]

Barraclough overstates the case. Particularly east of the Elbe, the aristocracy preserved and even expanded its privileges in the eighteenth century, chiefly at the expense of the peasantry. At the regional and local levels, the aristocracy remained "next to an economic and social also a

---

[40] Woloch, 26-30.

[41] Barraclough, 375.

[42] Barraclough, 377.

[43] Barraclough, 381.

first-rate political power," according to Grimminger.[44] Rarely could the princes govern without taking the clergy and aristocracy, the town oligarchies, and the territorial diets into account. Well into the eighteenth century, the state continued efforts to break what Grimminger calls "the parochial and essentially still feudal will of the dominant estates."[45]

Isolated as it was from the corporative mainstream, the new bourgeoisie supported efforts to subvert it. The new entrepreneurs lobbied to break corporative monopolies on industry and labor, and the bureaucracy, whether state or private, tended to be poorly paid, highly educated, and therefore open to liberal reform. Furthermore, many professionals and civil servants had bad memories of serving in aristocratic households as private tutors.[46] The state bureaucracy implemented liberal policies designed by territorial governments to undermine the power of the estates. As long as the state and the new bourgeoisie shared a common interest in weakening corporative privilege, they tended to converge in a common articulation and implementation of Enlightnment policies intended to centralize power at the expense of the estates.

But this policy cost the state a measure of its traditional legitimacy. The princes' efforts to subordinate the estates were what Barraclough calls "revolutionary acts implying a breach with the established order."[47] Where the state succeeded in centralizing power and thereby preserving its territorial integrity, it tended to lose internal legitimacy as it encroached on estates' rights. "The Hapsburg Empire [Brabant uprising, 1789-1790], France, and the American colonies," Norman Hampson notes, "offer the most striking but not the only examples of conflict arising from the determination of royal governments to provide themselves with new sources of revenue at the expense of the formerly privileged."[48]

---

[44] The aristocracy remained "neben einer ökonomischen und sozialen auch eine politische Macht ersten Ranges." Grimminger, 75.

[45] "... den partikularen und im Kern noch feudalen Willen der herrschaftsständischen Korporationen." Grimminger, 74.

[46] Fritz Valjavec, *Die Entstehung der politischen Strömungen in Deutschland 1770-1815* (Kronberg: Athenaeum; Düsseldorf: Droste, 1978), 82.

[47] Barraclough, 323.

[48] Norman Hampson, *A Cultural History of the Enlightenment* (New York: Pantheon Books, 1968), 180.

Of course, the "formerly privileged" were not the ones who dumped tea into Boston harbor or stormed the Bastille: in America, artisans, farmers, and intellectuals led the revolt, while in France the urban underprivileged carried the revolutionary banner. In Germany, where the revolt against tyranny was largely limited to literature, it was the new bourgeoisie that led the onslaught. Invoking "age-old endowments, contracts, rights ... two, three hundred years old," the scribe Vansen in Goethe's *Egmont* (1787) appeals to a traditional corporative constitution in building revolutionary sentiment against the Spanish state.[49] Why did a new bourgeoisie that participated in undermining estates' rights ultimately appeal to those same rights to attack state authority?

Grimminger offers an attractive explanation. The state conducted its revolution from above against the old order in the name of the Enlightenment. In order to survive, it needed to break the power of the estates, supplanting traditional obedience to authority with enlightened self-discipline on the part of each individual. The process of civilization required moving the locus of control from a traditional authority without (*Obrigkeit*) to psychological processes within. The new bourgeoisie participated in this project with an explosion of literature devoted to personal morality and self-reflection. Socially and politically, it joined in attacking the privileges of the estates in hopes of replacing them with what Grimminger calls "reason from below."[50] It strove to overcome its disenfranchisement within the corporative order by developing a new political system based on natural law, equal rights, and popular participation in government. In exchange for self-discipline, it sought to transform subjects into citizens.

By the late eighteenth century, such hopes had been dashed. Despite destroying what Grimminger calls "the social freedom of the whole corporative sphere of life," the state offered no constitutional guarantees of individual liberty to replace lost corporative freedoms.[51] Instead, the logic of absolutism disenfranchised all citizens absolutely.[52] Particular-

---

[49] "... uralten Stiftungen, Kontrakten und Gerechtigkeiten... von zwei-, dreihundert Jahren her." Johann Wolfgang Goethe, *Egmont* (Munich: DTV, 1975), 23 and 25.

[50] Grimminger uses the redundancy "rationalistische Vernunft von unten" Grimminger, 79.

[51] Although "die soziale Freiheit der gesamten ständischen Lebenswelt" was sacrificed, one found "keinen Ersatz für den Verlust an Gesamtfreiheit." Grimminger, 83.

[52] Grimminger sees "gehorsamspflichtige und politisch entmündigte Unter-

ly in Prussia, where top officials came from an aristocracy accustomed to unquestioning obedience, the state was loath to treat ordinary subjects as citizens with rights. The Enlightenment promise to situate authority within the private citizen was broken, discrediting the Enlightenment project. Frustrated and disillusioned, the new bourgeoisie abandoned Enlightenment ideals and again embraced the only seeming alternative: the traditional values and freedoms of corporative society.

With the erosion of traditional estates' rights, and particularly with the growth of censorship in the late eighteenth century, the new bourgeoisie experienced its continued disenfranchisement under Enlightened absolutism as a loss of freedom under state tyranny. In 1769, Lessing vented his anger in a letter to Christoph Friedrich Nicolai:

> Don't dare tell me of your freedom in Berlin to think and to write. It consists solely of the freedom to peddle as many forays against religion as one likes.... But just let ... somebody come along in Berlin who raises his voice on behalf of the subjects, against exploitation and despotism, as happens now even in France and Denmark, and you will soon see which land is to this day the most slavish in Europe.[53]

While the Prussian state allowed writers the freedom to attack traditional institutions such as the church, by 1769 this was not enough. Lessing calls for the freedom to criticize state tyranny itself. His primary target is no longer the clergy, but rather a state that not only exploits and oppresses its subjects, but punishes them for objecting. The Enlightenment's search for individual liberty culminated in conflict with the state.

By the late eighteenth century, the new bourgeoisie found itself ostracized in various ways from German society. In form and function, it belonged to no traditional estate, and its interests were pitted against

tanen" in a "Gesellschaft von Privatleuten." Grimminger, 74.

[53] "Sonst sagen Sie mir von Ihrer Berlinischen Freiheit zu denken und zu schreiben ja nichts. Sie reducirt sich einzig und allein auf die Freiheit, gegen die Religion so viel Sortisen zu Markte zu bringen, als man will.... Lassen Sie es aber doch einmal ... Einen in Berlin auftreten, der für die Rechte der Unterthanen, der gegen Aussaugung und Despotismus seine Stimme erheben wollte, wie es itzt sogar in Frankreich und Dänemark geschieht, und Sie werden bald die Erfahrung haben, welches Land bis auf den heutigen Tag das sclavischte Land von Europa ist." Letter of 25 August 1769 to Nicolai, in *Lessings Werke*, ed. Carl Christian Redlich (Berlin: Gustav Hempel, 1869), XX, 330.

corporative privilege. The court's relative openness to the new bourgeoisie between 1680 and 1740, which had been instrumental in developing its belief in the possibility of secular happiness, began to close after 1720, particularly with the accession of Frederick II to the Prussian throne in 1740. With rising censorship and the growing exclusivity of the court, the new bourgeoisie found itself increasingly at odds with the state and its agents in army and administration. As Enlightened absolutism spread in Germany especially after the Seven Years' War, and as the territorial states succeeded in centralizing authority, the net effect was to isolate the new bourgeoisie both socially and politically.

The new bourgeoisie faced a crisis of identity in the late eighteenth century. Non-corporative in character, this new sector found itself isolated from the traditional mainstream while facing growing repression from an increasingly hostile state. At the same time, its market orientation and domination of German letters opened new horizons and the means to explore them in public. A dialectic between social and political isolation and cultural opening and discovery informed the experience of the late eighteenth-century literary public.

In this context, a problem facing writers was the question of social identity: who were they and where did they belong? In exploring this question, their literary discourse often commented directly or indirectly on the contemporary conflicts and social processes that shaped and limited their possibilities. How did literature deal with the isolation of the new bourgeoisie from the social and political mainstream? What possibilities did the new bourgeoisie discover in the incipient processes of modernity?

Much of this experience was expressed in terms of natural spaces. The storm outside the tower in Gerstenberg's *Ugolino* delimits the experience of his characters; Goethe's Werther wanders from garden to spring to stormy cliffs; and Schiller's Karl finds refuge in the forest. In all three works, nature offers metaphorical space for exploring both alternative identities on the margins of society and the problem of isolation itself. How are natural spaces represented and explored in these works? To what extent do they appear frightening or destructive? These are the key questions of my study. The answers to them may offer insight into encoded attitudes towards problems of social isolation and new identity encountered by the eighteenth-century reading public.

Of course, the language of nature had not always expressed alternative social identities. Traditionally, its role was often the opposite: to stave off latent challenges to the status quo by excluding them from discourse. In the century between Gryphius and Haller, the cultural codes that informed the concept of nature underwent a dramatic change. In epistemological terms, this change can be described as a transition from metaphysics to empiricism: individual experience came to replace abstract principles as the measure of reality. Since this transition paved the way for the expression of modern experience as natural space, I shall discuss it next before analyzing the literary discourse of nature in the late eighteenth century. While the transition from metaphysics to empiricism was a complex and lengthy process, it can be summarized in terms of the debate that followed a pivotal event in eighteenth-century Europe: the earthquake that demolished Lisbon in 1755.

2

The Lisbon Earthquake

ON THE MORNING OF November 1, 1755, an earthquake estimated at between 7 and 8 on the Richter scale ripped through the city of Lisbon. Shock waves and tsunamis left large portions of the Portuguese capital in shambles. Fires raged for six days, leaving only 3,000 of 20,000 houses in central Lisbon habitable. 30,000 to 70,000 people died in the flooding, flames, and rubble. Thousands more were killed across Iberia and North Africa, and shocks were reported as far away as Stuttgart, the Netherlands, and Schleswig-Holstein.[1]

Eyewitness journal accounts spread the news of Lisbon's destruction to Germany within days. "Hereupon there was no lack of reflections from the God-fearing, of consolations from the philosophers, of admonishing sermons from the clergy," observed Goethe.[2] Johann Christoph Gottsched's *Das Neueste aus der anmuthigen Gelehrsamkeit* of December 1755 reprinted an anonymous poem on the earthquake's horrors from the *Leipziger Zeitung* of December 6, 1755; Gottsched himself added that the earthquake was God's judgment on a wicked humanity.[3] Friedrich Carl von Moser drew similar conclusions in his essay "Lissabon

---

[1] Charles Davison, *Great Earthquakes* (London: Thomas Murphy & Co, 1936), 4; O. Reinhardt and D. R. Oldroyd, "Kant's Theory of Earthquakes and Volcanic Action," *Annals of Science* 40 (1983), 248.

[2] "Hierauf ließen es die Gottesfürchtigen nicht an Betrachtungen, die Philosophen nicht an Trostgründen, an Strafpredigten die Geistlichkeit nicht fehlen." Johann Wolfgang Goethe, *Dichtung und Wahrheit, Goethes Werke*, ed. Erich Trunz (Munich: Beck, 1981), IX, 30.

[3] In his 1958 study on the Lisbon earthquake's effect on philosophy, Arthur Kemmerer describes this and other contemporary reactions to the disaster. Arthur Kemmerer, "Das Erdbeben von Lissabon in seiner Beziehung zum Problem des Übels in der Welt" (Diss. Frankfurt, 1958), 20.

1755."[4] Johann Rudolph Anton Piderit published a philosophical treatise on the earthquake's ramifications for the problem of evil. In 1756, the Schleswig scientist Joachim Francken completed a study on the physical origins of the earthquake. In the same year, the Leipzig theologian Rudolph Friedrich von Wichmannshausen published his reflections on the earthquake designed to promote religious revival.[5] From 1756 to 1758, Immanuel Kant wrote several tracts on the earthquake's physical origins and philosophical implications.[6] The flood of journal reports, pamphlets, scientific studies, sermons, poetic works, and philosophical discourses inspired by the Lisbon earthquake was unprecedented following a natural disaster.

Why all this interest in a disaster that affected Germany hardly at all? Although safely ensconced in Copenhagen, Friedrich Gottlieb Klopstock wrote to his parents that "[t]he great European earthquake ... has also made a great impression here, as you can well imagine."[7] Why does Klopstock refer to it not as the "Lisbon" or even "Portuguese" earthquake, but as "the great European earthquake"? And how could he assume that his parents in rural Saxony could easily imagine its impact on distant Denmark? What was it about the Lisbon earthquake that aroused such universal concern?

---

[4] Friedrich Carl von Moser, "Lissabon 1755," in his *Moralische und politische Schriften* (Frankfurt: Gebhard, 1763), I, 179-188.

[5] Johann Rudolph Anton Piderit, *Freye Betrachtungen über das neuliche Erdbeben zu Lissabon* (Marburg: 1756); Joachim Francken, *Versuch in physischen Betrachtungen über die Ursache und Entstehungsart des Erdbebens* (Schleswig: 1756); Rudolph Friedrich von Wichmannshausen, *Betrachtungen über das außerordentliche Erdbeben zu gegenwärtigen Zeiten, zur Erweckung an Gott, die Welt und an sich selbst hierbey zu gedenken, aufgesetzt* (Leipzig: 1756). Kemmerer describes all three works.

[6] Immanuel Kant, "Von den Ursachen der Erderschütterungen, bei Gelegenheit des Unglücks, welches die westlichen Länder von Europa gegen Ende des vorigen Jahres betroffen hat," *Königsberger Wöchentliche Frage- und Anzeigungs-Nachrichten*, 24 and 31 January 1756; "Fortgesetzte Betrachtung der seit einiger Zeit wahrgenommenen Erderschütterungen," *Königsberger Wöchentliche Frage- und Anzeigungs-Nachrichten*, April 1756; *Geschichte und Naturbeschreibung des Erdbebens am Ende des Jahres 1755*, published as a 40-page pamphlet 11 March 1758 by the Königsberg publisher Hartung.

[7] "Das große Europäische Erdbeben ... hatt [sic] hier wie Sie wohl dencken können, auch viel Eindruck [gemacht]." "An Anna Maria und Gottlieb Heinrich Klopstock," 26 or 28 December 1755, in *Friedrich Gottlieb Klopstock, Briefe 1753-1758*, ed. Helmut Rigge and Rainer Schmidt (Berlin: de Gruyter, 1988), 30.

Perhaps the most obvious explanation is the sheer magnitude of the disaster itself. However, earthquake disasters had surpassed the one at Lisbon in extent of destruction and number of victims at Villach (1348), Abruzzes (1456), Bénévent (1688), Naples and Sicily (1693), and the central Apennines (1703).[8] The 1693 disaster in Naples and Sicily alone claimed twice as many victims and struck what was once one of Europe's key commercial crossroads. In 1693, the region was still heavily populated and retained considerable commercial and agricultural wealth and clout; but when disaster struck, few outside Italy seemed to notice. Yet in 1755, when disaster befell Lisbon under similar circumstances, it caused a furor across Europe. Why the discrepancy?

The Rise of Optimism

The magnitude of the Lisbon disaster is not enough to explain widespread German interest in it. What happened and where it happened seem fairly comparable between the disasters of 1693 and 1755, but what is plainly different is when it happened. The first account of the Lisbon disaster to reach Germany helps to show what was changing:

> On All Saints Day, at nine o'clock in the morning, there was felt throughout all Portugal and especially in the capital city of Lisbon an earthquake as terrible as ever in any part of the world. This city, which was the richest in all Europe, which supplied all nations with diamonds, where almost nothing but gold was in vogue, is now nothing but a pile of stones under which more than 10,000 people were buried alive.... The earthquake happened right after a hurricane that caused a terrible sea, which swelled the Tajo unbelievably high. At the same time, doors burst and jumped from their hinges; walls and window bays also collapsed.... Wherever one turned, one saw houses collapse and under their ruins a countless number of people buried. Yes, if one had maintained all of one's senses and wits in the face of this reversal of the whole of nature, one could have imagined no place of safety, since one beheld death on all sides with open

---

[8] James Cornell describes the 1693 disaster in Naples and Sicily in *The Great International Disaster Book* (New York: Charles Scribner's Sons, 1976), 115. Theodore Bestermann discusses the other disasters referred to here in his "Voltaire et le désastre de Lisbonne," *Studies in Voltaire and the Eighteenth Century* 2 (1956), 11.

eyes.... This terrible destruction occurred in less than ten minutes.[9]

This account blends the old with the new: empirical description stands side by side with at least two traditional topoi. The account's exaggeration appears designed to evoke the wheel of fortune topos with the implicit message that pride goes before the fall. The earthquake is depicted as the most horrific ever; Lisbon is a city of legendary wealth; the disaster turns Lisbon into rubble burying countless victims. This revolution of nature fits the topos of a world turned upside down, with the allegorical message that death teaches the futility of seeking security in this world. Implicitly, the reader is invited to learn from the disaster to turn to the next.

However, this allegorical interpretation of the Lisbon disaster sharply conflicts with the writer's persistent references to empirical reality. The account is painstakingly set in real historical time: the earthquake happened on All Saints Day at nine o'clock in the morning and lasted under ten minutes. The location extends beyond Lisbon throughout Portugal. The number killed is not countless after all, but rather more than 10,000 (a conservative estimate). The writer attempts to explain natural phenomena (the flooded river) in terms of natural causes (a hurricane).

In this empirical context, the earthquake as reversal of nature takes on a whole new meaning. Instead of traditional allegory, it describes observed events. The naturally firm earth quakes, the natural water level rises high into the sky, and the naturally high buildings crumble to the ground, all of which amounts to an observed reversal of nature's physi-

---

[9] "Am Tage Allerheiligen, des Morgens um 9 Uhr fühlte man durch ganz Portugal und hauptsächlich in der Hauptstadt Lissabon ein solches erschreckliches Erdbeben, als jemals in irgend einem Weltheile gewesen ist. Diese Stadt, welche die reichste in ganz Europa war, welche alle Nationen mit Diamanten versahe, wo fast nichts als Gold im Schwange gieng, ist gegenwärtig nichts, als ein Steinhaufen, worunter mehr als 10,000 Menschen lebendig begraben worden.... Das Erdbeben erfolgte gleich nach einem Orkan, welcher ein erschreckliches Seewasser verursachte, das den Tajo unglaublich hoch aufschwellte. Zu gleicher Zeit borsten die Hausthüren und sprangen aus ihren Angeln; auch die Mauern und Erker stürzeten ein.... Wohin man die Augen wendete, sahe man Häuser einstürzen und unter derselben Ruinen eine unzählbare Menge Menschen begraben. Ja, wenn man bey dieser Umkehrung der ganzen Natur, bey vollen Sinnen und Verstand geblieben wäre, so hätte man keinen Ort der Sicherheit ausdenken können, da man den Tod von allen Seiten mit offenen Augen sahe.... Diese erschreckliche Verwüstung ist in weniger als 10 Minuten geschehn." *Gesammelte Nachrichten von dem Erdbeben der Stadt Lissabon*, ed. I. H. R. (Frankfurt, Leipzig: 1756), quoted in Kemmerer, 15.

cal properties. Next to the mythical thinking that informs his account of the Lisbon disaster, the writer displays the detached distance of an empirical observer. This empirical interest was shared by Kant and other scientists who drew on such accounts to study the earthquake's physical origins.

But there is a third layer of meaning here as well. The Lisbon earthquake signifies not just a temporary physical reversal of nature in Lisbon alone, but a reversal of the whole of nature. Even the traditional thought of life everlasting offers little comfort: one cannot imagine safety anywhere, presumably not even in the hereafter. The earthquake's reversal of nature deprives the writer of any sense of security at all, secular or spiritual, a thought so deeply disturbing that it threatens his sanity. Somehow, the disaster contradicts the whole idea of God, and this may be why it caused so much concern. But how could this have happened?

Traditionally, disasters were viewed as divine retribution for sin. If the innocent suffered, then perhaps it was due to their worldly ways, as a lesson to survivors, to atone for original sin, or to prepare their immortal souls for life everlasting in the hereafter. Whatever the reason, it was deemed consistent with divine Providence. The significance of events was not of this world, but of the next, and therefore disaster, war, pestilence, and other blights on humanity were seen as part of God's plan.

But in the first half of the eighteenth century, divine Providence came to measure what Goethe called "a world accustomed to peace and tranquility."[10] From 1715 to 1740, there was peace as well as economic and political stability in Europe. The mercantilistic and Enlightenment policies of Germany's princes favored and strengthened the new bourgeoisie, encouraging commercial expansion and travel.

As the new social sectors explored the political and economic space open to them, they took a growing interest in the empirical world and its history, an interest that infused the literary discourse they came to dominate. Travelogues and journals focusing on the changing experience of the moment and the empirical depiction of detail proliferated. Johann Gottfried Schnabel's novel *Insel Felsenburg* (1731-1743) typifies the Robinsonades that explored the characteristics and usefulness of flora and fauna on mythical shores. Barthold Heinrich Brockes's lyric collection *Irdisches Vergnügen in Gott* (1721-1748) portrays minute

---

[10] "...eine in Frieden und Ruhe schon eingewohnte Welt." Goethe, *Dichtung und Wahrheit. Aus meinem Leben*, in *Goethes Werke*, ed. Erich Trunz (Hamburg: Wegner, 1955; rpt. Munich: Beck, 1981), IX, 29. All references to Goethe's *Dichtung und Wahrheit* are from this edition.

details of nature in the name of God's greater glory. Through its literary discourse, the new bourgeoisie defined its relationship to nature in ever more secular, empirical terms, and it lent legitimacy to the new relationship by positing God's wisdom and benevolence increasingly in terms of the real world, fundamentally revising the traditional view of an inscrutable Providence oriented toward the hereafter. Divine Providence was increasingly seen to have ordered the cosmos to serve human secular interests.[11]

By mid-century, this notion developed into a philosophy known as "optimism," based on perhaps the most influential philosophical text of its time: Gottfried Wilhelm von Leibniz's *Theodicy* (1710). Drawing on *Genesis* and the principle that God is perfect, Leibniz reasoned that God created the most perfect universe possible. On the first day, He created the heavens and earth; on the next, day and night. This left Him with the choice of filling time and space with infinitely many possible worlds. Since God is perfect, he must have chosen the best world possible.[12]

Nothing about this argument is particularly unconventional. On its face, it jibes well with the traditional view of this world as a vale of tears. The best world possible could easily be a world of calamity in which the devout prepare themselves for the next.

However, it was articulated in a time hungering for moral and religious justification of its growing secularism. Perhaps the strongest secularizing influence was exercised by the moral weeklies, periodicals of moralizing and didactic content in short genres. Appearing in the 1720s, they flourished from 1740 to 1760, especially in the Protestant north and east and in the cities. They were instrumental in shaping the literary public of the late eighteenth century.[13]

The moral weeklies adapted Leibniz's philosophy to their own secular purposes. In the early 1750s, for instance, *Der Mensch* argued that the human being should develop a native ability to reason and reflect:

> By constitution, man is a rationally free being and should therefore, through his own reflection and through the use of his

---

[11] As Jacob Viner notes in *The Role of Providence in the Social Order* (Princeton: Princeton UP, 1972), 12.

[12] Georg Wilhelm von Leibniz, *Die Theodizee*, trans. and ed. Artur Buchenau (Leipzig: Feliz Meiner, 1925), 101.

[13] Wolfgang Martens, *Die Botschaft der Tugend* (Stuttgart: Metzler, 1968), 147.

powers in accordance with nature, learn to know properly himself, the world, and God, and should act according to this knowledge and thereby promote his salvation to the greatest possible extent.[14]

Despite the appeal to God, there is little concern here with the afterlife. The focus is on knowing oneself, the world, and God, in that order of priority. Both happiness and salvation depend on cultivating a use of human faculties in accordance with nature, which in turn leads to knowing God. The emphasis is on living in this world, not the next.

One corollary of this sort of thinking was bound to make enemies in the clergy. If man can find happiness by virtue of his own makeup in accordance with nature, then the road to salvation no longer necessarily leads through the spiritual mediation of the Church. "He who knows nature, knows God," *Der Freygeist* intoned in 1745; "he who knows God, honors Him; he who honors Him, follows His laws; he who follows His laws is virtuous; and he who is virtuous finds salvation."[15] Nature is believed to reveal God and His laws, a notion derived from Leibniz's argument: if God's creation is as perfect as possible, then it must reveal His own perfection, wisdom, and benevolence. If so, then exploring nature must lead not only to happiness, but to spiritual salvation (*Glückseligkeit* connotes both).

The moral weeklies not only inflated the value of the secular world and its empirical exploration, they went so far as to condemn traditional religiosity. "Our enjoyment," *Der Menschenfreund* declared in 1747,

> remains so pleasing to the Highest Being, and to us so proper, that we resist God's views and our own nature when we are discontent and agitated. Do not trust those who always complain about the misery of life, who dream of constant calamities, and

---

[14] "Der Mensch ist, seiner Bestimmung nach, ein vernünftig freyes Wesen und soll also durch sein eigenes Nachdenken, und durch einen der Natur gemäßen Gebrauch seiner Kräfte, sich selbst, die Welt und Gott richtig kennen lernen, und nach dieser Erkenntniß handeln und dadurch seine Glückseligkeit aufs möglichste befördern." *Der Mensch* (Halle: Johann Justinus Gebauer, 1751-1756), quoted in Martens, 231.

[15] "Wer die Natur kennt, der kennt Gott; wer Gott kennt, der ehret ihn; wer ihn ehret, der erfüllet seine Gesetze; wer seine Gesetze erfüllet, der ist tugendhaft; und wer tugendhaft ist, der ist glückselig." *Der Freygeist* (Leipzig: Christlob Mylius, 1746), quoted in Martens, 218.

who regard the world as a dungeon in which we have been placed for our torment.[16]

The reasoning here again draws on Leibniz while secularizing him. Since physical creation is as perfect as possible, the pursuit of happiness in it is dictated by our very nature. Conversely, a traditionally long-suffering view of creation contradicts our nature and God's purpose. This argument belittles the medieval view of this world as full of trials and tribulations intended to prepare the soul for the next.

While the conflict between modern secularism and medieval spiritualism can be traced at least to the writings of Cardinal Nicholas of Cusa (1401-1464),[17] it was restricted to an elite few until the eighteenth century. Through the moral weeklies, arguments against abandoning secular pursuits in favor of salvation after death gained popular currency. Such arguments were designed to lend spiritual legitimacy to the growing secular interest of the new bourgeoisie. They grafted an emphasis on the physical nature of creation onto Leibniz's theodicy in order to maintain that the pursuit of secular happiness was God's ultimate purpose. If the best of possible worlds was consistent with physical creation, then divine Providence could be empirically observed in the workings of nature itself. By the time of the Lisbon earthquake, a German reading public weaned on moral weekly literature had come to reject the vale-of-tears philosophy of preceding centuries and to expect secular happiness in a universe rationally ordered by a wise, omnipotent, and benevolent Creator.

The Lisbon disaster deeply confounded these expectations. Lisbon's destruction seemingly refuted the thesis that God's benevolence was observable in nature's workings. The shock of Lisbon is eloquent testimony to the degree to which secularism had supplanted traditional religiosity within the German literary public by 1755.

The crisis that followed the Lisbon disaster has sometimes been raised to mythical proportions. Many assume that Leibniz's optimism entails the belief that things will turn out well, as opposed to pessimism.

---

[16] "Unser Vergnügen bleibt dem höchsten Wesen so gefällig, uns aber so anständig, daß wir den Ansichten Gottes und unserer eigenen Natur widerstreben, wenn wir mißvergnügt und unruhig sind. Trauet denen Menschen nicht, welche immer über das Elend des Lebens zu klagen haben, die von beständigen Unglücken träumen, und welche die Welt als einen Kerker betrachten, worinn wir zu unserer Plage geleget worden." *Der Menschenfreund* (Jena: Johann Wilhelm Schaubert, 1748), quoted in Martens, 266-267.

[17] As Hans Blumenberg points out in *The Legitimacy of the Modern Age*, trans. Robert M. Wallace (Cambridge and London: MIT Press, 1983), 483-547.

Since the Lisbon disaster spawned attacks on philosophical optimism, some have concluded that it must have given way to pessimism or skepticism in the disaster's wake.[18]

However, there is little evidence to suggest that after the Lisbon earthquake, Europeans started believing that natural or historical events would probably turn out badly. The eighteenth-century debate sparked by the Lisbon disaster was not over optimism versus pessimism, but over deeper issues. French Jesuits coined the term "optimism" when they disparaged Leibniz for restricting God's freedom while rationalizing the existence of evil.[19] What troubled the Jesuits was the potential in Leibniz's theory for affirming this world instead of the next, a potential realized by the moral weeklies. The debate over optimism was not over whether things would turn out well or not, but over whether one should focus on things in this world or instead forsake them for the next. The Lisbon disaster sharpened this debate, ultimately liberating the secular, empirical implications of optimism from the constraints of its rationalist precepts.

In what follows, I will attempt to show that the furor following the Lisbon earthquake was only part of a long-drawn process of redefining the relationship to nature in terms of individual experience rather than metaphysical principle. I will start by discussing the rationalist precepts at the core of optimist philosophy. Then I will examine the crisis of rationalism in the wake of the Lisbon disaster.

The Metaphysics of Optimism

Alexander Pope articulates the fundamental principles of philosophical optimism in his *Essay on Man* (1736). Pope begins his *Essay* with the axiom that God in His infinite wisdom must have created the best world possible. This poses a problem, since some creatures are more

---

[18] Variations of this argument are made by Hans Seligo, "Das große Erdbeben," *Merian* 12 (1959); Theodore Bestermann; Wilhelm Lütgert, *Die Erschütterung des Optimismus durch das Erdbeben in Lissabon* (Gütersloh: Bertelsmann, 1928); and Harald Weinrich, "Literatur eines Weltereignisses: das Erdbeben in Lissabon," *Literatur für Leser*, ed. Harald Weinrich (Stuttgart: Kohlhammer, 1971). While Arthur Kemmerer argues that optimism soon recovered from the shock of Lisbon, he too poses the problem as one of optimism versus pessimism, overlooking the deeper conflict between rationalism and empiricism.

[19] In the *Journal de Trévoux ou Mémoires pour servir a l'histoire des sciences et des arts* (1737). *Historisches Wörterbuch der Philosophie*, Vol. 6, col. 1240.

perfect than others: angels are more perfect than man, who in turn is judged more perfect than animals. If God created the most perfect world possible, why are some creatures less perfect than others?

Pope solves this problem by positing a "great chain of being." If plenitude is better than uniformity, perfection requires the greatest variety of creatures possible, and since nothing is missing from a perfect world, these creatures must be ordered on a continuous scale of perfection.[20] By definition, the principles of plenitude and gradation inform the best of possible worlds. Therefore, imperfection in its particulars is a necessary part of creation's overall perfection. Eliminating evil would, as Pope puts it, "in the full creation leave a void, where, one step broken, the great scale's destroy'd."[21]

After positing first principles, Pope spends most of his *Essay* proving them. He calls on the reader to notice a mounting scale of perfection in mental powers (the principle of gradation) in the broad range of God's creatures (the principle of plenitude). His evidence ranges from "the mole's dim curtain, and the lynx's beam" to "instinct" in the "grov'ling swine" and the "half-reasoning elephant" that is man.[22] Formally, Pope's reasoning is empirical: he draws on the particulars of experience in order to explain reality. However, in doing so he leaps from empirical observation to metaphysical justification of already posited principles. Pope appeals to the senses to affirm truths rationally deduced from metaphysical axioms adduced a priori.

On the other hand, Pope's *Essay* contains numerous passages depicting the rich variety of natural phenomena in sensual images, from the "green myriads in the people grass" to the "warbles through the vernal wood" and the "spider's touch, how exquisitely fine."[23] By invoking an ultimately religious theme (God's great scale of creation), Pope can depict the perceived attributes of physical phenomena in a way that may not have appealed to German audiences a century earlier. The illustration of the principles of plenitude and gradation lends legitimacy to both an aesthetic, non-allegorical portrayal of experienced nature and an incipient empirical methodology. Similarly, the moral weeklies explored the secular world and its empirical phenomena in the name of

---

[20] Arthur O. Lovejoy explains this thesis in *The Great Chain of Being* (Cambridge: Harvard UP, 1953), 208-226.

[21] Alexander Pope, *Essay on Man*, ed. A. Hamilton Thompson (Cambridge: Cambridge UP, 1913), 12 (Ep. 1, lines 243-244).

[22] Pope, 11 (Ep. 1, lines 207-222).

[23] Pope, 11 (Ep. 1, lines 210-217).

piety. By blending and even confusing secular and spiritual themes, philosophical optimism fostered a growing interest in worldly pursuits and pleasures.

This marriage of convenience between rationalist metaphysics and empirical interest was fraught with inherent tension. Pope's *Essay* contradicts its own rationalist faith in man's power to reconstruct the universe through reason. A key passage in the *Essay* maintains that particular evil is really universal good, since what man mistakenly calls nature, chance, and discord are really art, direction, and harmony designed by God. Therefore, in spite of erring reason, "one truth is clear, whatever is, is right."[24] But if the art, direction, and harmony of creation are unseen by man due to erring reason, then it seems impossible to leap from empirical observation to the metaphysical certainty that partial evil is really universal good. Pope not only acknowledges limitations on the power of reason to reconstruct reality, he limits knowledge to experience. "The bliss of man...," he says, "is not to act or think beyond mankind," since human powers to understand the universe are limited to man's nature and condition.[25] Pope's recognition that knowledge is limited to experience explains the formal empiricism of his argumentation while subverting the universal truths he deduces from metaphysical principles.

Pope's contemporaries further developed the empirical implications of optimist philosophy. In his *Treatise on Human Nature* (1740), David Hume challenged the rationalist assumption that a priori knowledge can divulge the secrets of nature. The only basis of practical conduct, Hume argues, is "the experienced train of events." Understanding cannot surpass empirical boundaries, even if the imagination must.[26]

As early as 1745, the German philosopher Christian August Crusius questioned Leibniz, maintaining that as far as we know, God might have made a better world. While God must have made a world that is very good, the thesis that it is the best world possible is unverifiable.[27] In wanting to compare the evidence before concluding that creation is as perfect as possible, Crusius implicitly argues that knowledge of the world is limited to finite experience of it.

---

[24] Pope 13 (Ep. 1, lines 289-294).

[25] Pope, 10 (Ep. 1, lines 189-190).

[26] David Hume, *A Treatise of Human Nature*, ed. L. A. Selby-Bigge (Oxford: Clarendon Press, 1896), 142.

[27] Christian August Crusius, *Entwurf der nothwendigen Vernunft-Wahrheiten* (1745; rpt. Hildesheim: Georg Olms, 1964), 743 (par. 385).

In his *Venus physique* (1745), Pierre-Louis Moreau de Maupertuis derided the kind of thinking that leaps from the particulars of experience to metaphysical precepts. "One constructs for oneself a satisfactory system while one is ignorant of the characteristics of the phenomenon to be explained," he maintains. "As soon as these are known, one sees the inadequacy of one's reasoning and the system fades away."[28] Maupertuis argues that experience measures reality, since empirical measurement reduces metaphysical systems to absurdity.

In 1753, as President of the Berlin Academy of Sciences, Maupertuis called for papers on Pope's maxim, "Whatever is, is right." According to Johann Christoph Gottsched, Maupertuis hoped to discredit both Pope and Leibniz.[29] Four treatises were submitted, including one by Gottsched and another jointly by Gotthold Ephraim Lessing and Moses Mendelssohn. The only one to attack the basic principles of philosophical optimism was written by Adolf Friedrich von Reinhard.[30] Not surprisingly, Maupertuis awarded it the prize.

By the time of the Lisbon earthquake in 1755, scholars across Europe were challenging the metaphysical basis of philosophical optimism. Still, even though the wars of 1740-1748 may have shaken faith in optimism,[31] before the shock of Lisbon there was no clear crisis of confidence in it. Instead, there were spreading doubts.

Even the Lisbon disaster failed to demolish optimism. Some writers seized the opportunity to attack the secularism implicit in optimist philosophy; others reiterated old arguments in defense of divine Providence; only a few challenged the rationalist metaphysics behind philosophical optimism. I will briefly discuss the first two tendencies before moving on to what seems to me the heart of the matter: the empirical challenge to rationalist metaphysics. Critics of rationalism included Voltaire, Jean-Jacques Rousseau, Immanuel Kant, Johann Georg Hamann, and Johann Gottfried Herder. While the Lisbon disaster changed few minds right away, it contributed to the ultimate triumph in Germany of what, for lack of a better word, I call empiricism: the accep-

---

[28] Pierre-Louis Moreau de Maupertuis, *Venus physique* (1745), as quoted in Hampson, 77.

[29] Gotthold Ephraim Lessing, *Gesammelte Werke* (Berlin: Aufbau-Verlag, 1956), VII, 255 (footnote 6).

[30] Adolph Friedrich von Reinhard, *Abhandlung über die Lehre von der besten Welt*, (Leipzig: Christian August Wichmann, 1757).

[31] Hampson, 88.

tance of individual experience rather than revealed or rationally deduced principles as the primary criterion of reality.

Onslaught Against Optimism

In the eighteenth century, most Europeans still believed "that by the shuddering of the supposedly solid ground beneath their feet they were supernaturally commanded to listen in dread and shame to the holy voice of God," as T. D. Kendrick puts it.[32] The disaster reinvigorated the medieval view that natural events have supernatural causes. "Learn, O Lisbon," the Jesuit priest Gabriel Malagrida exhorted in a popular pamphlet, "that the destroyers of your houses, palaces, churches, and convents ... are your abominable sins and not comets, stars, vapors and exhalations, and similar natural causes."[33] Dozens of minor shocks in the months following the disaster fanned fears of yet a greater earthquake to come, one that would finish God's work of obliterating Lisbon. Measures designed to appease an angry God included special penitential processions of Lisbon's top clergy and officialdom, led by Portugal's royalty.

However, these measures were deemed insufficient by prophets like Malagrida, who called on Lisbon's population to abandon reconstruction and instead devote all its energy to penitence under clerical guidance. "There must be no mistake about the seriousness or urgency of Malagrida's case," Kendrick observes. "If God watched Lisbon, scourge in hand, what could anyone possibly find to do more important than to placate His wrath by the exercise of true repentance?"[34] Lisbon's secular authorities were alarmed by Malagrida's teachings. Intent on avoiding panic and repairing the damage, they favored natural explanations of the earthquake. Malagrida was imprisoned as a heretic and executed by the Inquisition in 1761, and his pamphlet was banned.

Across Europe, the Lisbon disaster fanned the flames of a similar conflict between medieval spiritualism and modern secularism. Voltaire describes how Pope's *Essay* was already under fire from clerics who objected that if whatever is, is right, then human nature has not been corrupted, and there is no need for Redemption mediated by the

---

[32] T. D. Kendrick, *The Lisbon Earthquake* (London: Methuen & Co, 1956), 1.

[33] Gabriel Malagrida, *Juizo da verdadeira causa do terremoto* (Lisbon: 1756), trans. and quoted in Kendrick, 137-138.

[34] Kendrick, 90.

Church. Defending Pope's "excellent poem" against such attacks, Voltaire notes with satisfaction that they had only increased its sales and success.[35]

However, the Lisbon earthquake provided German traditionalists with new arguments. Gottsched branded the earthquake God's angry judgment against Lisbon for its "vanity and blasphemy."[36] Klopstock called the disaster God's warning to Europe to desist from debauchery.[37] A poem in the *Frankfurter Gelehrten Zeitungen* of April 16, 1756 tied Lisbon's fate to that of Sodom.[38] This view of earthquakes and their moral causes and cures sharply conflicted with practical remedies proffered by some, such as sinking shafts to prevent pressures from building in subterranean caverns.[39] Such notions were wrong, the traditionalists argued, because nature was not self-referential, but pointed beyond itself to a higher spiritual order in God.

In 1756, Johann Rudolph Anton Piderit developed this argument when he noted that a whale had been sighted off Lisbon eight days before the earthquake. Had the citizens of Lisbon but remembered the story of Jonah, whose sermon rescued a huge city from disaster, they might have averted the earthquake by repenting and turning to God. With his allegorical whale, Piderit reiterates the traditional view of nature as encoded Scripture pointing beyond itself to a transcendent order in God. Such arguments were designed to undermine the contemporary focus on the experience of the senses and recover lost ground for the notion that this world should be spiritually abandoned for the next.

Although thrown on the defensive by the Lisbon disaster, the proponents of philosophical optimism soon responded. In his 1756 poem on the earthquake, Johann Peter Uz claims that "raving prophets' tongues" only add to the woe of Lisbon's destruction. Uz asks his muses to let his "countenance be cheerful not just on sunny days."

---

[35] Voltaire, Preface to his "Poème sur le désastre de Lisbonne," in *The Works of Voltaire*, trans. William F. Fleming (New York: E. R. DuMont, 1901), X:2, 5-6. All references to Voltaire's "Poème" are from this edition.

[36] Johann Christian Gottsched, *Das Neueste aus der anmuthigen Gelehrsamkeit*, December 1755, quoted in Kemmerer, 55.

[37] Klopstock, *Briefe, 1753-1758*, 30.

[38] Quoted in Kemmerer, 51-52.

[39] Suggested by a "Professor Holtmann" in the *Göttinger Gelehrten Anzeigen*, 14 February 1756, cited in Kemmerer, 108.

> Even when the earth shakes
> The divine thought must glimmer on my forehead
> That virtue is happy and my soul lives
> Even under whole worlds' ruins![40]

These lines cultivate the notion that reality is shaped by human perspective and activity. God is reduced to a thought that appeals to the senses (it "glimmers"), while happiness and salvation derive from virtue no matter what happens in the world. Therefore, whatever is, is right. Uz edited a poem he wrote in 1754 on the theodicy several times after the Lisbon disaster without modifying its claim that "whatever happens always happens for the best."[41] He returns to this theme in his odes to cheerfulness (1756-1758), concluding that "whatever is, is right, but in a context that I cannot fathom, nor ask to."[42]

Immanuel Kant joined the battle against optimism's religious opponents following the Lisbon disaster. In his *Geschichte und Naturbeschreibung des Erdbebens am Ende des Jahres 1755* (1756), which discusses the Lisbon earthquake's natural origins, Kant calls the view of the earthquake as God's revenge on sinners a cruel slight to its victims. He attacks the anthropomorphization of nature implicit in the idea that disasters are divine retribution for sin, insisting that man cannot guess God's purposes in the world. Human knowledge is limited to empirical inquiry of the sort Kant himself undertakes. Any attempt to leap beyond the particulars of experience is doomed, and therefore the view of the Lisbon disaster as God's angry judgment is mistaken.

Nevertheless, Kant maintains that earthquakes are ultimately beneficial, since they deposit ore in the ground and minerals in the atmosphere while creating hot springs and exuding warmth. "Whatever damage the cause of earthquakes may have created for man on the one

---

[40] "Laß mein Antlitz heiter seyn,/Nicht bloß zu sonnenvoller Tagen./... Es müss' auf meiner Stirn, wann schon die Erde bebt,/Der göttliche Gedanke schimmern,/Daß Tugend glücklich ist und meine Seele lebt,/Auch unter ganzer Welten Trümmern!" Johann P. Uz, "Das Erdbeben," *Sämtliche poetische Werke von J. P. Uz*, ed. A. Sauer (Stuttgart: Nendeln/Liechtenstein, 1968), 150 (number 66, lines 25-36).

[41] "...was geschieht, aufs beste stets geschieht." Johann Peter Uz, "Theodizee," *Werke*, ed. Sauer, 138 (number 63, line 78).

[42] "Was ist, ist alles recht, doch im Zusammenhange,/Den ich nicht einzusehn vermag, auch nicht verlange." Johann Peter Uz, "Versuch über die Kunst, stets fröhlich zu seyn," *Werke*, ed. Sauer, 262 (Third Letter, lines 333-334).

hand," he declares, "it can easily replace for him with gain on the other."[43] Like Pope before him, Kant displays the contradiction inherent in philosophical optimism between its latent empiricism and its rationalist metaphysics: while rejecting the arguments of his religious opponents on the grounds that man cannot fathom God's higher purposes, he rationalizes the suffering at Lisbon in the name of divine Providence.

Structurally, the arguments of optimists like Kant were similar to the traditional ones they were designed to refute. Both deduced reality from metaphysical principle, justifying Lisbon's destruction in terms of God's higher purpose. From a traditional viewpoint, God's judgment of Lisbon showed His benevolence by teaching humanity to turn away from secular interests and seek spiritual salvation instead. From an optimist perspective, the Lisbon disaster reflected divine Providence in enhancing the world's resources and contributing to the good of the whole. Both arguments anthropomorphize nature while rationalizing human suffering.

Kant was quick to point out the cruelty of viewing the Lisbon earthquake as divine retribution. Ironically, Voltaire turned this argument against philosophical optimism in his "Poème sur le désastre de Lisbonne" (1755): optimism's view of the disaster as necessary for the greater good makes cruel mockery of those maimed under Lisbon's ruins. Voltaire subtitled his poem "An Inquiry into the Maxim, 'Whatever is, is Right,'" hinting that he considered it a late contribution to Maupertuis's 1753 Berlin Academy of Sciences competition on Pope's *Essay*. For Voltaire, a demolished Lisbon offers incontrovertible evidence that Pope's rationalizations of evil are wrong.

Voltaire had grown skeptical of rationalist metaphysics well before the Lisbon earthquake. In 1738, he published a tract on Newtonian physics in which he expresses doubt that knowledge transcends the limits of the senses. "From the stars to the earth's center," he writes, "in the external world and within ourselves, every substance is unknown to us. We see appearances only; we are in a dream."[44] Reality is not a metaphysical system independent of human perception. As it exists for us to know, it is a chain of being from celestial bodies to earth's core

---

[43] "Was auch die Ursache der Erdbeben den Menschen auf einer Seite jemals für Schaden erweckt hat, das kann sie ihm leichtlich auf der anderen Seite mit Gewinnst ersetzen." Immanuel Kant, *Geschichte und Naturbeschreibung des Erdbebens am Ende des Jahres 1755*, in *Immanuel Kants Sämmtliche Werke*, ed. G. Hartenstein (Leipzig: Leopold Voss, 1867), I, 440. All references to Kant's *Geschichte* are from this edition.

[44] Voltaire, *Traité de metaphysique* (1738), quoted in Hampson, 76.

that ultimately ends within us. Like dreams, what we see is governed by human powers of perception and creation. Influenced by Newton, Voltaire turns the traditional great chain of being on its head: instead of deducing it from metaphysical principles, he begins to induce it from the experience of the senses.

This incipient questioning of metaphysics led Voltaire to doubt Pope's maxim, "Whatever is, is right." In 1746, almost ten years before the Lisbon disaster, he concluded a fable with the words, "If all is not well, all is passable."[45] While questioning the belief in a best of possible worlds, Voltaire continued to accept the proposition that God must have made a world that was at least tolerable.

After the Lisbon disaster, Voltaire abandoned this view, bitterly attacking Pope in his "Poème." He begins with a stark portrayal of bodies piled high and limbs crushed under rubble, then asks how this evidence of suffering can be squared with rationalist philosophy:

> Say, when you their piteous, half-formed cries,
> Or from their ashes see the smoke arise,
> Say, will you then eternal laws maintain,
> Which God to cruelties like these constrain?[46]

Voltaire frames his poem as a debate between "you," an imaginary adversary who defends rationalism, and "me," a poetic voice hardly removed from the author's own. One by one, he refutes the arguments that "you" raise in defense of rationalism.

His first target is the argument that the Lisbon disaster is divine retribution against sinners. Since innocent children died in Lisbon while lust flourishes unpunished in Paris, this argument must be false. Those who abstract from concrete suffering to draw moral lessons from the disaster are guilty of inhumanity. Nor is suffering to be born in meek silence with Job: "cruel fate" and "the snares of death ... suffer me from complaint to find relief."[47] Voltaire insists on the right not only to recognize one's secular fate for what it is — a mediation of the senses, of pain and grief — but to criticize and even challenge it. By appealing to humanity, he defines reality in terms of human perception, activity, and feeling. Man moves from the outer fringes of a metaphysical cosmos to fill center stage in an empirical one.

---

[45] Voltaire, *Le monde comme il va* (1746), quoted in Hampson, 92.

[46] Voltaire, "Poème," trans. Fleming, X:2, 8.

[47] Voltaire, "Poème," trans. Fleming, X:2, 9.

Having thus disposed of traditional religiosity, Voltaire devotes the rest of his poem to the argument that particular evils are necessary to the greater good. Not all events, he insists, are requisite in the broad scheme of things. Some, such as the dust raised by a coach's wheels, are irrelevant to the course of events. Even if a few people benefit from the suffering of others, there is no obvious reason why this should be so. Why should God not steer events such that nobody suffers and everybody benefits?

This argument stresses the priority of empirical evidence over abstract reasoning in evaluating the course of events. Voltaire insists on projecting reality in terms of human perception and feeling, to the point of rendering an anthropomorphic God. "But I can feel, my heart oppressed demands," he writes, "aid of that God who formed me with His hands."[48] By our very nature, because we can feel, we must demand aid from God. A feeling humanity presupposes a merciful God whose pitying eye disposes Him to aid those in trouble. By envisioning a humane God, Voltaire verges on defining the Creator in terms of His creation, a position that anticipates Ludwig Feuerbach.

However, Voltaire never goes so far as openly to question the traditional concept of God. Although he insists that the experience of the senses refutes metaphysical speculation as to final causes, he stops short of Pierre Bayle's systematic skepticism. Instead, the theodicy remains for him an insoluble problem:

> Mysteries like these can no man penetrate,
> Hid from his view remains the book of fate.
> Man his own nature never yet could sound,
> He knows not whence he is, nor whither bound.

Knowledge is limited to human experience, which cannot transcend the realm of the senses. "The human mind derives all its knowledge from experience," Voltaire declares in a footnote; "no experience can give us an insight into what preceded our existence, into what is to follow it, nor into what supports it at present." Voltaire compares questions about the ultimate ground of being to "the vulgar proverb: Was the hen before the egg, or the egg before the hen?"[49]

But instead of dismissing such questions as sophisms, Voltaire takes them seriously. Even though "human wisdom ... is utterly at a loss with

---

[48] Voltaire, "Poème," trans. Fleming, X:2, 13.

[49] Voltaire, "Poème," trans. Fleming, X:2, 17.

regard to first principles of things without supernatural assistance,"[50] this does not mean that there are no such first principles. Beyond human experience lies an inscrutable realm of truth and consolation in God. Voltaire arrives at this conclusion by process of elimination. He offers four possible solutions to the problem of the theodicy, three of which he refutes. He dispatches the view of sinners in the hands of an angry God with the observation that God is just and merciful. Nor is God the *deus ex machina* supposed by optimist philosophers, since He "can't be enchained" by nature's laws. The Manichaean vision of evil despite God's will contradicts the notion of God's omnipotence. This leaves one possibility: "this transient world" is "but a passage that conducts to God." While in it, we cannot explain our sufferings; we can only hope that "death will land us on a happier shore."[51]

This answer to the problem of the theodicy is close to the traditional Christian notion of silent long-suffering in this vale of tears. In an apparent about-face, Voltaire finally embraces the story of Job that he at first seems to question. "The light of truth I seek in this dark state," he declares, "[a]nd without murmuring submit to fate." "This state," or secular reality, is "dark" in a dual sense: it is full of undeniable suffering, and the final causes of suffering must remain unknown. All one can do is submit to fate and hope for relief in the hereafter. "All may be well; that hope can man sustain, All now is well; 'tis an illusion vain."[52] Voltaire bluntly dismisses the secular orientation implicit in optimist philosophy, abandoning all hope of succor in this world in favor of the next.

This conclusion highlights an apparent contradiction in Voltaire's poem. Voltaire unquestionably defines reality in terms of human experience: knowledge of the world is limited to human perception and feeling. Nevertheless, he espouses a traditional Christian faith in a realm "on happier shores." The metaphysical underpinnings of his argument signify far less of a break with philosophical optimism than commonly thought. A perceptive reviewer in the *Göttingische Gelehrten Anzeigen* of November 22, 1759 notes that the poem only appears to contradict optimism while actually affirming its underlying religious principles.[53] Voltaire's argument is akin to J. P. Uz's appeal to everlasting life under

---

[50] Voltaire, "Poème," trans. Fleming, X:2, 17.

[51] Voltaire, "Poème," trans. Fleming, X:2, 15.

[52] Voltaire, "Poème," trans. Fleming, X:2, 18.

[53] *Göttingische Anzeigen für gelehrte Sachen* 140 (1759:#2), 1216.

Lisbon's ruins or the young Goethe's claim that God preserves the immortal soul despite the Lisbon calamity.[54] The metaphysical component to Voltaire's argument is shared with the very philosophy of optimism it is designed to demolish.

Nevertheless, Voltaire's contribution to the rise of empirical discourse and the demise of rationalism should not be overlooked. Voltaire liberates the discourse of nature from subservience to metaphysics. In defining knowledge of the world in terms of human perception and feeling, he consigns metaphysics to the realm of faith at best, spurious speculation at worst. Perhaps nowhere does he make this point more effectively than in the closing lines of *Candide*:

> Pangloss used now and then to say to Candide, "There is a concatenation of all events in the best of possible worlds; for, in short, had you not been kicked out of a fine castle...; had you not been put into the Inquisition; ... had you not lost all your sheep..., you would not be here to eat preserved citrons and pistachio nuts." "Excellently observed," answered Candide, "but let us take care of our garden."[55]

Pangloss's speculation may be excellently observed, but it does not "take care of our garden." Metaphysics becomes irrelevant in the practical discourse of daily life. Pope's *Essay* may have been the last gasp of the medieval *ordo* ideal integrating all aspects of reality, secular and spiritual, empirical and metaphysical. After Voltaire, it became increasingly difficult to maintain.

Empirical Approaches: Rousseau, Kant, Hamann, Herder

Even before the Lisbon earthquake, Jean-Jacques Rousseau developed a critical concept of nature in his *Discours sur l'origine de l'inégalité* (1754). Rousseau attempts to show that inequality is a social product, not a natural one. In the course of history, humanity moves through several stages to a "fatal enlightenment of civil man" characterized by the philosophy of Enlightenment rationalism.[56] In his original condition,

---

[54] *Goethes Briefwechsel mit einem Kinde*, ed. Gustav Konrad (Cologne: Bartmann, 1960), 272.

[55] Voltaire, *Candide*, in *The Works of Voltaire*, trans. Fleming, I, 208.

[56] Jean-Jacques Rousseau, *Discourse on the Origin of Inequality*, in *The First and Second Discourses*, trans. Roger D. and Judith R. Masters (New York: St.

man measures reality in terms of perception and feeling governed by instinct and tempered by reason. Philosophical rationalizations of human woe, on the other hand, corrupt the natural ability to empathize with human suffering.

By implication, Rousseau criticizes the precepts behind philosophical optimism in two ways. First, rational philosophy is not an original way of measuring reality, but a historically derived one functioning to engender vanity, or enhance self-interest. Second, the philosopher's own natural tendency to define reality in terms of human feeling revolts within him against his metaphysical rationalizations of suffering.[57] The original human response to reality is to interpret it in terms of human perception and feeling rather than a historically derived metaphysics. Rousseau's *Discours* develops an incipient empirical epistemology.

After the shock of Lisbon, Rousseau apparently retreated from this position, embracing rationalist philosophy instead. He wrote a long rebuttal to Voltaire's "Poème" in the form of a letter dated August 18, 1756. Written with an eye to publication, the letter reaffirms Pope's maxim, "Whatever is, is right." Maintaining that an omniscient and omnipotent God must have created the best world possible, Rousseau strikes at the fundamental inconsistency in Voltaire's "Poème:" his continued subscription to a metaphysical notion of divine Providence despite his insistence on the empirical limits of knowledge. Since Voltaire concedes that God is perfect, wise, powerful, and just, he must draw the logical conclusion and grant that His creation is as perfect as possible.

Despite its rationalist gist, Rousseau's letter contributes to empirical discourse. After criticizing Voltaire's supposed atheism, Rousseau concedes that arguments for or against atheism are inconclusive "because they concern things about which men have no real idea."[58] This coincides with Voltaire's conclusion that metaphysical truths exceed the limits of empirical knowledge and are therefore unverifiable. Ultimately, metaphysics are a matter of faith, not knowledge.

While Voltaire appeals to divine revelation to resolve the problem of the theodicy, Rousseau looks within. He distinguishes between reason,

---

Martin's Press, 1964), 150.

[57] Rousseau, *Discourse*, trans. Masters, 132.

[58] "...parce qu'elles roulent sur des choses dont les hommes n'ont aucune véritable idée." Jean-Jacques Rousseau, "Letter to Voltaire on Providence," in *Rousseau: Religious Writings*, ed. Ronald Grimsley (Oxford: Clarendon Press, 1970), 45. All references to Voltaire's "Letter to Voltaire" are from this edition.

which governs verifiable knowledge, and the soul, the locus of metaphysical certainty, or faith. Faith, he says, is not a matter of choice, since the soul cannot subsist in doubt, but is irresistibly drawn to the hope of higher truths.[59] Like Voltaire, Rousseau distinguishes between empirical and metaphysical knowledge, and he acknowledges that the latter is inaccessible through reason. But he goes a step further: he transforms metaphysical knowledge into a process of personal confession. In personalizing metaphysics, Rousseau projects divine Providence in terms of his own inner experience. In so doing, he breaks with Voltaire's traditional division of knowledge into physical and metaphysical components, the latter inaccessible except through divine revelation. Instead, man becomes the measure and agent of all things, whether secular or spiritual.

Rousseau does more than undermine the rationalist precepts behind philosophical optimism: he stimulates optimism's inherent process of secularizing metaphysics while spiritualizing nature. But Rousseau contributes to an empirical discourse of nature in yet another way. He points out that society, not nature, is responsible for where and how Lisbon was built. The disaster could have been avoided if Lisbon had been built elsewhere or differently, or had people in its aftermath been more charitable and less greedy.[60]

This insight transfers the problem of evil from metaphysics to history.[61] By focusing on the social rather than metaphysical implications of the Lisbon disaster, Rousseau obviates the whole chicken-and-egg question of the theodicy that stumped Voltaire. Natural events are intrinsically neither helpful nor harmful to man. Their good or evil stems primarily from how society is organized.

Rousseau implicitly discredits the key premise of philosophical optimism here: an anthropomorphic nature. Pope's maxim that "whatever is, is right" projects nature as inherently good. In view of their readership's orientation toward secular self-improvement, the moral weeklies interpreted and popularized nature's inherent goodness in terms of a divine design calculated to benefit humanity. It was thought that nature reflected divine Providence because it contributed to human well-being. The Lisbon earthquake proved so shocking because it seemed to contradict this belief. In his "Poème," Voltaire eloquently voices the contradiction.

---

[59] Rousseau, "Letter to Voltaire," ed. Grimsley, 45-46.

[60] Rousseau, "Letter to Voltaire," ed. Grimsley, 33-34.

[61] As Harald Weinrich notes. Weinrich, 75.

Rousseau argues that there is no contradiction because the disaster stemmed from human activity, not nature. In arguing that evil derives not from nature, but from social history, Rousseau returns to a position consistent with his *Discours* of 1754. From an optimistic standpoint, Rousseau's argument throws out the baby with the bath water: if evil is a product of social history, then good must also derive from history, not nature. And if nature cannot be said to be inherently beneficial to humanity, then there may be no contradiction between divine Providence and violent nature, but there is no longer any reason to believe that "whatever is, is right." Deprived of any intrinsic goodness or design, nature becomes purely self-referential, while evil loses its inevitability and becomes corrigible through social change. In stripping nature of its anthropomorphism, Rousseau not only challenges the basis of optimist philosophy, he begins to articulate the objective distance from observed events critical to an empirical discourse of nature. At the same time, he opens the door to a revolutionary social critique that helped usher in, according to Goethe, "those tremendous world changes in which everything existing seemed to perish."[62]

From January to April 1756, Immanuel Kant published three short scientific studies on the origins of the Lisbon earthquake. The second of these, *Geschichte und Naturbeschreibung des Erdbebens*, castigates those who assume that whatever happens is designed to reward or punish humanity. "Whatever provides comfort and enjoyment in the world," Kant declares, "that, one imagines, exists only for our own sake, and nature undertakes no changes that cause any inconvenience to man except to discipline, threaten, or take revenge on him."[63] Human utility, Kant argues, cannot be said to be the final cause of the natural order. The earthquake benefits (hot springs, ore deposits, atmospheric minerals, and warmth) that he adduces to ameliorate the shock of Lisbon do not suffice, he concedes, to prove that this is the best of possible worlds. "The reasons that I have given ... are, of course, not of the type that provide the greatest conviction and certitude." Instead,

---

[62] "...jene ungeheuere Weltveränderungen, in welchen alles Bestehende unterzugehen schien." Goethe, *Dichtung und Wahrheit*, ed. Trunz, IX, 488.

[63] "Was in der Welt zur Bequemlichkeit und zum Vergnügen gereicht, das, stellt man sich vor, sei blos um unsertwillen da, und die Natur beginne keine Veränderungen, die irgend eine Ursache der Ungemächlichkeit für den Menschen werden, als um sie zu züchtigen, zu drohen, oder Rache an ihnen auszuüben." Kant, *Geschichte*, ed. Hartenstein, I, 442.

they are at best "suppositions."[64] Kant not only distinguishes here between empirical and metaphysical truths, he doubts whether empirical observations can provide metaphysical certainty. He questions the very basis of optimism's anthropomorphic view of nature, suggesting a beginning break with its rationalist precepts.

Even before Rousseau, Kant transfers the problem of evil from metaphysics to history, describing the Lisbon disaster as a social problem rather than a philosophical one. While earthquakes inevitably happen, he argues, it is unnecessary to build large, easily damaged structures in earthquake zones. In a reference to the earthquake-prone Pacific rim, Kant claims that Peruvians build structures unlikely to cause severe damage and great carnage in the event of an earthquake. By implication, he suggests that similar construction techniques in Europe might have prevented the Lisbon earthquake from turning into a disaster.

Kant takes issue with Voltaire's fatalistic resignation to evil on earth. "I am far from indicating...," he insists, "that man is subject to an inexorable fate of natural laws without recourse to his particular advantages." Communities can learn from disasters to prevent future ones. "When a city or a country becomes aware of the harm with which divine Providence terrifies it or its neighbors; is there still then any question which side it should take in order to forestall the ruin that threatens it?" The side to be taken is divine Providence, and the argument that faith in God can avert disaster is quite conventional. However, choosing sides means more for Kant than faith in God: it means acting as historical subject to avert disaster. "A prince who, motivated by a noble heart," he declares, "lets himself be moved by this anguish of the human race to avert the misery of war ... is a salutary instrument in the benevolent hand of God...."[65] In implicitly appealing to Frederick II of Prussia to avert the impending conflagration of the Seven Years' War, Kant ties the Lisbon

---

[64] "Die Gründe, die ich ... angeführt habe, sind freilich nicht von der Art derjenigen, welche die größeste Überzeugung und Gewißheit verschaffen." They are "Muthmaßungen." Kant, *Geschichte*, ed. Hartenstein, I, 442.

[65] "Ich bin weit davon entfernt, hiemit anzudeuten, als wenn der Mensch einem unwandelbaren Schicksal der Naturgesetze, ohne Nachsicht auf seine besonderen Vortheile, überlassen sei.... Wenn eine Stadt oder ein Land das Unheil gewahr wird, womit die göttliche Vorsehung sie oder ihre Nachbarn in Schrecken setzt; ist es denn wohl noch zweifelhaft, welche Partei sie zu ergreifen habe, um dem Verderben vorzubeugen, das ihnen droht? ... Ein Fürst, der, durch ein edles Herz getrieben, sich [durch] diese Drangsale des menschlichen Geschlechts bewegen läßt, das Elend des Kriegs ... abzuwenden ... ist ein wohltätiges Werkzeug in der gütigen Hand Gottes...." Kant, *Geschichte*, ed. Hartenstein, I, 444-445.

disaster to contemporary politics. Not only does he transform an instance of violent nature into a metaphor for social and political choices, he uses it to propagate his own pacifism in perhaps one of the first symbolic uses of violent nature imagery as a discourse on social and political developments.

After his *Geschichte*, Kant staunchly defended optimism. In a letter to J. G. Lindner dated October 28, 1759, he scorned Daniel Weymann's essay "De mundo non optimo" (1759) for attacking Pope and Leibniz. Perhaps provoked by Voltaire's *Candide*, he then wrote his *Versuch einiger Betrachtungen über den Optimismus* (1759), intended to refute not only Weymann, but also Christian August Crusius (the German philosopher who had questioned Leibniz's theodicy in 1745) and Adolph Friedrich von Reinhard (who submitted the winning essay in Maupertuis's 1754 Berlin Academy of Sciences competition on Pope's *Essay*). There is little trace here of the doubts about rationalist metaphysics in Kant's *Geschichte*.

However, the theodicy remained a gnawing problem for Kant. In 1763, he attempted to reconcile empirical evidence with metaphysical truth in *Der einzige Beweisgrund einer Demonstration des Daseins Gottes* by divorcing a priori (intuitive) from a posteriori (empirical) knowledge. Kant's demonstration of God's existence is ontological: nothing could be conceived to exist without God; therefore, because something conceivably exists, God's existence is self-evident. Kant explicitly distinguishes this ontological proof of God from attempts to derive divine Providence from nature, or God's creation. "All proofs that proceed from [God's] workings to His existence as their origin can ... never make the nature of this necessity comprehensible."[66] Kant now sees such attempts, presumably including those in his own *Geschichte*, as misguided. "It is quite necessary," he claims, "for one to be convinced of God's existence; but it is not as necessary for one to demonstrate it."[67] By strictly differentiating between empirical knowledge of the world and intuitive knowledge of God, Kant implicitly challenges the rationalist

---

[66] "Alle Beweise, die sonsten von den Wirkungen [Gottes] auf sein, als einer Ursach Dasein geführt werden möchten, als sie es nicht tun, können niemals die Natur dieser Notwendigkeit begreiflich machen." Immanuel Kant, *Der einzige Beweisgrund einer Demonstration des Daseins Gottes, Immanuel Kant, Werke*, ed. Wilhelm Weischedel (Frankfurt: Suhrkamp, 1968), II:2, 653.

[67] "Es ist durchaus nötig, daß man sich vom Dasein Gottes überzeuge; es ist aber nicht eben so nötig, daß man es demonstriere." Kant, *Beweisgrund*, ed. Weischedel, II:2, 738.

premise that knowledge of the world of the senses ultimately derives from metaphysical principles.

Three years later, in *Träume eines Geistersehers* (1766), Kant abandons rationalist epistemology altogether. As "wisdom's companion," he declares, philosophy delineates the limits of empirical knowledge. "But when one finally arrives at basic conditions, then the business of philosophy is finished, and: how something could be a cause or have power is impossible ever to see through reason, but rather these relations must be taken only from experience."[68] Knowledge of the external world is based solely on experience. Physics and metaphysics do not mix, since reason offers no insight into the experience of the senses.

Kant scorns rationalist philosophers such as Christian Wolff, calling them "dreamers of reason." "All such conclusions," he declares, "such as those that state how my soul ... stands in relation to other beings of its kind now or in the future can never be anything more than fictions...."[69] This was a slap at Pope, whose *Essay* places man in relation to God, angels, and other spirits in the great chain of being. Such metaphysical speculation now seems to Kant pure invention, the product of an overheated imagination. "Let us accordingly leave all noisy doctrines on such distant subjects to the speculation and care of idle heads," he concludes, "and so I close with what Voltaire finally has his honest Candide say after so many useless scholastic quarrels: let us attend to our happiness, go into our garden, and work."[70]

The very arguments Kant used in his *Geschichte* and *Versuch* to defend philosophical optimism now seem to him useless. By 1766, he had made a complete turnabout, abandoning optimist metaphysics in

---

[68] "Ist man aber endlich zu den Grundverhältnissen gelangt, so hat das Geschäfte der Philosophie ein Ende, und: wie etwas könne eine Ursache sein oder eine Kraft haben, ist unmöglich jemals durch Vernunft einzusehen, sondern diese Verhältnisse müssen lediglich aus der Erfahrung genommen werden." Immanuel Kant, *Träume eines Geistersehers*, in *Immanuel Kant, Werke*, ed. Weischedel, II:2, 985.

[69] "Alle solche Urteile, wie diejenige von der Art, wie meine Seele ... mit andern Wesen ihrer Art jetzt oder künftig in Verhältnis steht, können niemals etwas mehr als Erdichtungen sein...." Kant, *Geisterseher*, ed. Weischedel, II:2, 986.

[70] "Laßt uns demnach alle lärmende Lehrverfassungen von so entfernten Gegenständen der Spekulation und der Sorge müßiger Köpfe überlassen.... [U]nd so schließe ich mit demjenigen, was Voltaire seinen ehrlichen Candide, nach so viel unnützen Schulstreitigkeiten, zum Beschlusse sagen läßt: laßt uns unser Glück besorgen, in den Garten gehen, und arbeiten." Kant, *Geisterseher*, ed. Weischedel, II:2, 989.

favor of the empirical discourse of nature implicit in the closing lines of *Candide*. This reference to Voltaire suggests the Frenchman's importance in bringing Kant to rethink his own epistemological premises. Instead of deducing reality from metaphysical principles adduced a priori, Kant begins to critically describe its formation in the mind through categories of perception, reason, and judgment. The logocentric authority of the revealed word gives way in Kant's incipient critical philosophy to the authority of human faculties. Though opposed to Hume's skepticism, Kant came to espouse a broadly empirical focus on reality as the product of human experience synthesized from categories of the mind.

Johann Georg Hamann rarely addressed the Lisbon disaster directly.[71] However, in a letter to J. G. Lindner in October 1759, he bitterly attacked Kant's *Versuch* for exceeding the bounds of knowledge.[72] Kant's method of understanding, he argues, is precisely backwards: by deriving the particulars of experience from a conceptual whole, he explains what is known in terms of what is not. Implicitly, Hamann distinguishes between metaphysical and empirical knowledge. Only God knows the final causes of things, while human knowledge is limited to the fragmentary experience of nature and one's own inner feelings and motives.

Hamann soon addressed Kant personally with his criticisms. Apparently, Hamann and Kant had discussed collaborating on a physics study. In several letters toward the end of 1759, Hamann tells Kant that his theories about the cosmos are less useful than those in the Bible. Kant's rationalist epistemology cannot be used to explain nature, Hamann argues, because it logically deduces existence from timeless universals. A historical model like the story of creation in *Genesis*, artificial though it may be, is preferable to Kant's rationalism because it contains the origins of things. No matter how simplistically, it explains the world as a process of creation and evolution rather than metaphysical necessity.

In his third letter, Hamann explicitly attacks philosophical optimism, accusing Rousseau of contradicting himself in his letter to Voltaire.

---

[71] In a letter to his parents, Hamann refers to the Lisbon disaster as a kind of divine judgment. "An die Eltern," 21 January 1756, *Johann Georg Hamann: Briefwechsel*, ed. Walther Ziesemer and Arthur Henkel (Wiesbaden: Insel, 1955), I, 137 (number 56). In *Sokratische Denkwürdigkeiten*, Hamann mentions Voltaire's reaction to the Lisbon disaster. Johann Georg Hamann, *Sokratische Denkwürdigkeiten*, ed. Sven-Aage Jorgensen (Stuttgart: Reclam, 1968), 53.

[72] "An Johann Gotthelf Lindner," 12 October 1759, *Hamann: Briefwechsel*, ed. Ziesemer and Henkel, I, 425 (number 163).

Instead of subsuming the particular under the general as Rousseau does, Hamann advocates the opposite. Any universal is merely a construct of concrete particulars, just as an age is an arbitrary period of single days. It has no ontological reality beyond the particulars that comprise it. Therefore, the whole of creation can only be as good as its minutest particulars. To admit with Rousseau that particulars may be evil yet to insist that the whole is good is, Hamann argues, contradictory.

Next, Hamann addresses Kant's own defense of philosophical optimism in his *Versuch*.

> And if you want to give your listeners proof that the world is good, then do not point them to the whole, because nobody can grasp that, nor to God, for He is a Being that only a blind man can gaze upon, and only a vain person believes himself able to recognize His way of thinking and moral character.[73]

While Hamann does not deny that the world is good, he insists that no such conclusion can be drawn from metaphysical speculation. If God is known only to the blind, the final causes of things are inaccessible to empirical inquiry, just as the whole exceeds the empirical limits of knowledge. Therefore, the logical deduction that a benevolent God must have created a best of possible worlds is unverifiable. Implicit in Hamann's argument is a strict separation of empirical from metaphysical discourse: judgments about the world must be based on the experience of the senses, which offer no insight into the metaphysical nature of God. While Kant never responded to Hamann in writing, the epistemological revisions in his *Beweisgrund* and *Geisterseher* reflect similar points of view.

In his *Ideen zur Philosophie der Geschichte der Menschheit* (1784), Johann Gottfried Herder sharply criticizes what he calls Voltaire's "unphilosophical" reaction to the Lisbon disaster. Since humanity owes its existence to forces of nature that make the earth habitable, Herder argues, their occasional violence jibes with "eternal laws of wisdom and

---

[73] "Und wenn Du deinen Zuhörern einen Beweiß geben willst, daß die Welt gut ist; so weise sie nicht auf das gantze, denn das übersieht keiner, noch auf Gott, denn das ist ein Wesen, das nur ein Blinder mit starren Augen ansehen kann, und dessen Denkungsart und moralischen Charakter sich nur ein eitler Mensch zu erkennen zutraut." "An Immanuel Kant," 1759, *Hamann: Briefwechsel*, ed. Ziesemer and Henkel, I, 452. Kant's *Versuch* had announced a lecture series on philosophical optimism at Königsberg University during the winter semester of 1759.

order."[74] Herder's reasoning echoes Kant's enumeration of earthquake benefits in his *Geschichte*, or Pope's deduction of nature's perfection from God's wisdom and benevolence. Herder accepts the Christian view of God as benevolent, omniscient, and omnipotent, positing a great chain of being similar to Pope's: God has ordered everything "from the firmament to the grain of dust" to reflect "one wisdom, benevolence, and power."[75] He seems to defend philosophical optimism against Voltaire.

However, Herder's view of nature differs from Pope's in two key ways. First, Herder makes no mention of supernatural entities such as angels. His chain of being exists only in nature. While Pope uses the particulars of experience to illustrate metaphysical principles, Herder focuses on empirical particulars and natural processes.

Second, God's workings do not necessarily benefit humanity. Unlike Pope, Herder formulates the notion of divine Providence as a troubling question rather than a logical conclusion.

> Proud man is loath to regard his race as ... a progeny of the earth and as the spoil of all-consuming decay; and yet do not history and experience force this image on him? ... [A]nd yet man is evidently constituted to seek order, to look beyond one spot in the ages, to build posterity on the past: for this is why he has recollection and memory.[76]

In questioning the human tendency to project order and purpose onto the world, Herder implicitly challenges his own projection of divine

---

[74] "Es war ein unphilosophisches Geschrei, das Voltaire bei Lissabons Sturz anhob.... Was geschähe anders als was nach ewigen Gesetzen der Weisheit und Ordnung geschehen mußte?" Johann Gottfried Herder, *Ideen zur Philosophie der Geschichte der Menschheit. Herders Sämmtliche Werke*, ed. Bernhard Suphan (Berlin: Weidmannsche Buchhandlung, 1887), XIII, 24. All references to Herder's *Ideen* come from this edition.

[75] "Der Gott, der in der Natur Alles ... geordnet, ... so daß vom großen Weltgebäude bis zum Staubkorn ... nur eine Weisheit, Güte und Macht herrschet...." Herder, *Ideen*, ed. Suphan, XIII, 7.

[76] "Der stolze Mensch wehret sich, sein Geschlecht als eine ... Brut der Erde und als einen Raub der alles-zerstörenden Verwesung zu betrachten; und dennoch dringen Geschichte und Erfahrung ihm nicht dieses Bild auf? ... [U]nd doch ist offenbar der Mensch dazu geschaffen, daß er Ordnung suchen, daß er einen Fleck der Zeiten übersehen, daß die Nachwelt auf die Vergangenheit bauen soll: denn dazu hat er Erinnerung und Gedächtnüß." Herder, *Ideen*, ed. Suphan, XIII, 8.

wisdom and order onto nature. History and experience suggest that there is no perceptible divine plan to shape nature for the good of humanity as a whole. Instead, evidence suggests that humanity is merely the product of an unconscious nature that creates and destroys without apparent rhyme or reason. There is no hint here of a best of possible worlds in any anthropomorphic sense.

Herder finds this conclusion difficult to accept, because human faculties tend to abstract from particulars and organize the world systematically. Recollection and memory are designed to perceive historical patterns, tracing out God's plan in the world. Like Kant's concept of practical reason, this notion of reality shaped in the mind differs profoundly from traditional epistemology. For Pope, reality is shaped by God according to rational principles manifest in the human mind; for Herder, reality is shaped by humanity through powers that provide it with a distant facsimile of God's mysterious design in the world. Unlike Pope's, Herder's criterion of knowledge is not logical deduction from metaphysical principle, but rather the human faculty of organizing the empirical data of the past and present into historical patterns. "Whoever wants mere metaphysical speculations," he observes, "can obtain them more easily;"

> but, divorced from experiences and analogies of nature [as they are], I believe that they are an exercise in futility that seldom leads to the goal. God's process in nature, the thought that the Eternal One has actually presented to us in the series of His works: they are the holy book the characters of which I have deciphered and will continue to decipher, of course less well than an apprentice [might do] but at least with faith and enthusiasm.[77]

Herder measures reality in terms of history and experience or recollection and memory. In either case, man becomes the measure of all things. God's thoughts remain metaphysical categories that guide human inquiry, but they are accessible only with the help of empirical evidence, not through reasoning from abstract principles, and even then they are

---

[77] "Wer bloß metaphysische Spekulationen will, hat sie auf kürzerm Weg; ich glaube aber, daß sie, abgetrennt von Erfahrungen und Analogien der Natur, eine Luftfahrt sind, die selten zum Ziel führet. Gang Gottes in der Natur, die Gedanken, die der Ewige uns in der Reihe seiner Werke thätlich dargelegt hat: sie sind das heilige Buch, an dessen Charakteren ich zwar minder als ein Lehrling aber wenigstens mit Treue und Eifer buchstabirt habe und buchstabiren werde." Herder, *Ideen*, ed. Suphan, XIII, 9.

barely traceable. Herder differs from Pope in treating the goodness of creation not as a logical conclusion, but rather as a hypothesis to bear critical scrutiny in the light of historical evidence. His *Ideen* attempts to test this hypothesis by reading "the fate of mankind from the book of Creation."[78]

In the process, like Kant and Rousseau before him, Herder transfers the problem of evil from metaphysics to history, but with a difference: instead of identifying the Lisbon disaster as a social problem of where and how to build cities, he sees it as part of nature's history of cyclical creation and destruction. Historical change is the condition of existence; life and growth are predicated on devolution and death. Herder reformulates the whole problem of innocent suffering in a way that tends to eliminate it. If death and destruction are the conditions of life and creation in a constantly changing universe, then it makes little sense to label natural events either good or evil.

Herder's argument undermines the anthropomorphism of philosophical optimism in two ways. First, God's design in the world cannot be deduced from metaphysical principles such as divine Providence, but must be induced from historical inquiry into the particulars of experience. Second, historical inquiry does not support the proposition that nature is designed to serve human purposes. History and experience speak against it. Nature does not owe humanity its services; instead, humanity owes nature the habitat that supports it.

For Herder, Voltaire's resignation to evil on earth is "unphilosophical" because it imputes to nature and God human qualities and expectations. Underlying Voltaire's agitation over the Lisbon disaster is his unspoken expectation that a benevolent God must steer events to benefit humanity. Voltaire's anthropomorphic view of nature mirrors optimism's own, and to the extent that Herder attacks the former, he rejects the latter.

The Myth of the Lisbon Earthquake

The myth that the Lisbon earthquake shattered philosophical optimism pervades modern scholarship, despite evidence that optimism faced earlier challenges in Europe and persisted long afterward. Not optimism itself was at issue, but its metaphysical precepts; and these were discredited not by the events of 1755, but rather by the needs of the new bourgeoisie as it gradually discovered its public voice. The rich

---

[78] "...das Schicksal des Menschen aus dem Buch der Schöpfung." Herder, *Ideen*, ed. Suphan, XIII, 9.

nature imagery in Pope's *Essay* suggests that optimism itself helped open the door to a modern empirical discourse of nature. In response to the growing secular orientation of the incipient new bourgeoisie in a climate of traditional religiosity, Pope and others blended empirical and metaphysical elements in perhaps the last great attempt to formulate a comprehensive philosophical system in the tradition of medieval rationalism. Optimism's critics then drew on its own latent empiricism to attack its metaphysical basis.

Optimism's inner contradictions gradually sharpened as the new bourgeoisie outgrew its origins in the cradle of absolutism and sought the conceptual means to explore new horizons while challenging the metaphysical rationale of traditional society. In the 1720s, an empirical discourse of nature emerged alongside metaphysics within optimist philosophy itself; by 1766 (the year of Kant's *Geisterseher*), empiricism — in the broad sense of defining reality in terms of human perception, judgment, and activity — had displaced traditional metaphysics as the dominant discourse of nature in German letters. With its rationalist basis undermined, optimist philosophy waned in influence, even though it persisted as a residual formation in Germany well into the nineteenth century.

The conflict between the rationalist metaphysics of philosophical optimism and its own latent empiricism was already underway by the time of the Lisbon earthquake, and there is little reason to believe that it would have stopped without the shock of Lisbon. Nevertheless, the Lisbon disaster offered a focal point for the desultory debate over the metaphysical principles of optimism that lasted in Germany roughly from the 1740s into the 1780s. By 1770, after the additional shock of the Seven Years' War, the moral weeklies, once instrumental in spreading optimist philosophy, had all but disappeared.

Each in his own way, Voltaire, Rousseau, Kant, Hamann, and Herder contributed to the rising empirical discussion of nature and the decline of metaphysics in the late eighteenth century. The new discourse of nature contained several elements: it articulated knowledge of the physical world in terms of human faculties of perceiving, feeling, and organizing reality; it relegated metaphysics to (at best) the secondary role of defining the limits of understanding; it transformed the problem of evil from a metaphysical to a moral, social, or historical one, liberating social commentary and criticism from the strait jacket of religion; and it undermined the anthropomorphic depiction of nature, paving the way for its detached articulation as historical process. Redefined in this way, nature could be used to explore personality, individuality, and subjectivity, to propagate the priority of practical pursuits in the secular world, to express attitudes toward social change or the lack of it, and to support a scientific version of empirical inquiry. As I will show in the following chapters, German literature after the Lisbon earthquake developed the new discourse of nature into a way of articulating the concrete experience and aspirations of isolated individuals on the fringes of traditional corporative society: the new bourgeoisie.

3

Nature and Family in Gerstenberg's *Ugolino*

"THE STORY IN THIS play is familiar from Dante."[1] With these words Heinrich Wilhelm von Gerstenberg prefaces his play *Ugolino* (1767). Gerstenberg refers to the thirty-third canto of Dante's *Inferno*, Ugolino's tale of being locked by his adversary Ruggieri together with his sons in a tower to starve. His play is based on the contemporary appeal of Dante's "Ugolino" story.

Yet Gerstenberg goes well beyond Dante. References in his play to Count Ugolino as "liberator of Pisa" yet as "traitor" imply familiarity with sources other than Dante. The storm outside the tower, the escape attempt, utopian dreams of life outside, and conflicts among Ugolino's sons are all added to Dante's basic story line.

Apparently, it was not Dante, but something about the Ugolino story itself that fascinated contemporary audiences in Germany. Given the conventional importance of the preface in defining a play's purpose, Gerstenberg's brief introduction assumes new meaning if regarded less as a decorous bow to his illustrious predecessor than as a clue that his play deals with and comments on the Ugolino story's public appeal, its "familiarity from Dante." Gerstenberg may have chosen to dramatize the Ugolino tale in part because contemporaries saw themselves reflected in its characters, setting, and historical situation. Obviously, there was nothing common about being locked in a tower to starve; still, something about Ugolino's situation was true, it seems, to contemporary

---

[1] "Die Geschichte dieses Drama ist aus dem Dante bekannt." *Heinrich Wilhelm von Gerstenberg, Ugolino*, ed. Christoph Siegrist (Stuttgart: Reclam, 1966), 6. Since all references to Gerstenberg's *Ugolino* are from this edition, they are followed only by the page number in parentheses.

experience for it to have evoked such widespread interest. The tower of famine spoke somehow to contemporaries' perceptions of their own situation in Germany: in his review of the play, Herder notes that through the "deep inner knowledge of the human soul" reflected in it, Gerstenberg tells "our nation ... something extraordinary."[2] What is it about Ugolino's situation that spoke to contemporaries, and what does this say about contemporary attitudes toward social change in Germany?

The Endangered Family

For political reasons, Ugolino and his three sons are imprisoned in a tower on a stormy night to starve. Mentioned throughout the play, the storm is a constant reminder of outside threat to the intimate family circle. The world beyond the confines of the tower is populated by wicked people such as the prison guard who fails to bring food or Ugolino's rival Archbishop Ruggieri and his minions. When Francesco recounts the history of Ugolino's betrayal by Ruggieri, Anselmo replies, "Is that the world? Well, by the holy mother of God, I detest it!"[3]

By contrast, the world inside the tower appears warm and caring. Anselmo asks for food not for himself, but for his younger brother. The boys hug each other and sit on their father's lap. Anselmo proclaims a sense of family integrity within the tower, only wishing the Archbishop had imprisoned their mother too, "and we would have been a world of joy for each other."[4]

Two worlds square off in a conflict that frames the play and informs its characters. The intimate family circle inside the tower finds itself both isolated from and threatened by the world of social and political activity outside. The polarity of the situation underlines Ugolino's key problem: he and his family find themselves isolated from society in a life-threatening situation. Their survival depends on breaking out of their private-sphere prison, which requires open confrontation with adversaries in public. Read as a discussion of Ugolino's social isolation and possibilities of overcoming it, the play sheds light on contemporary

---

[2] "...daß sich in [den Empfindungen des Stücks] eine tiefe innere Kenntnis der menschlichen Seele äußere ... — daß ... ein Dichter ... spreche, der unsrer Nation in der Folge was Außerordentliches zusagt." Johann Gottfried Herder, "Ugolino," in *Allgemeine deutsche Bibliothek* 11 (1770), rpt. in *Gerstenberg, Ugolino*, ed. Siegrist, 75.

[3] "Ist das die Welt? Nun, bei der heiligen Mutter Gottes, ich verabscheue sie!" (18)

[4] "...und wir wären eine Welt der Freude füreinander gewesen." (14)

attitudes toward processes of social change in the late eighteenth century that led to the isolation of the new bourgeoisie.

Gerstenberg based his story on the thirteenth-century power struggle between Count Ugolino Gherardesca and Archbishop Ruggiero Ubaldini for control of Pisa. Ugolino led Pisa's navy in a disastrous trade war against Genoa, then used the ensuing crisis to seize absolute power. While Ugolino was away at his villa, Ruggiero launched a coup. He imprisoned the captured Gherardescas in a tower, then boarded it up when relatives could no longer pay ransom.[5] Gerstenberg was apparently struck by the feudal logic of retaliating against an entire clan to eliminate the threat posed by one member. A key element in the power struggle between Ugolino and Ruggieri in Gerstenberg's play is the tragedy of family demise.

Ugolino takes refuge from the horror of starvation by remembering his family past. In Act IV, he lifts Gaddo onto his lap and asks his sons to be cheerful. Then he recalls happier times when all Pisa celebrated Anselmo's birth. Francesco remembers Ugolino's great victory as another joyous occasion when personal success and public celebration went hand in hand. He tells how a jubilant procession met Ugolino at his country villa, where he awaited his wife and sons in triumph.

Anselmo's birth suggests the family's genesis in harmony with natural cycles at a time when special events in the private sphere were still public occasions. Ugolino's victory celebration at his country estate unites family and society in a bucolic setting. Ugolino relates this utopian vision of family unity in harmony with nature and society to what he calls a "higher life after death," which is much happier since "it has no variations."[6]

This ideal of family unity without variation implies that the problem facing the Gherardescas is conflict and change per se. Though cryptic and fragmented, shared memories of family coherence attempt to explain (literally, "make level" by removing incoherence) the present in terms of the past, to overcome the threat to family by grounding it in a mythical Golden Age. By remembering the past harmony between

---

[5] Robert Davidsohn, *Geschichte von Florenz* (Berlin: E. Siegfried Mittler, 1908), II:2, 253-264, 324-328. Gerstenberg adopts Dante's alteration of the historical Ruggiero's name to Ruggieri. Still, his play shares enough elements with the historical account (such as references to Ugolino's villa) to suggest that he was familiar with some version of it.

[6] "[D]as höhere Leben nach dem Tode" is "doch viel glücklicher" since "es hat keine Abwandlungen." (53)

private and public domains, their conflict in the present is ideally overcome.

However, the strategy of escaping conflict and change into the past proves futile: even while Ugolino and his sons imagine family coherence, family disintegration is graphically depicted on stage by Gianetta's coffin. Since utopias are fantasy resolutions of real-life conflicts and contradictions, Ugolino's remembered Golden Age implies that social isolation remains the key problem facing the intimate family circle. As an attempt to overcome family incoherence, the Gherardescas' family history actually reveals much about the nature of the conflict they face.

Gherardesca family history is traced in a series of recollected fragments that punctuate the play, beginning with Ugolino's memory of how Gianetta "lovingly and shyly ... sank into my arms." Curiously, this infuriates Ruggieri, whose "leaden, watery face raged with the storm of his soul."[7] Until then, Ugolino and Ruggieri had been friends. Ruggieri's anger focuses not on Ugolino personally, but on his establishment of a family with Gianetta.

While jealousy might seem a motive, nowhere is this stated. Instead, the dialogue suggests that what infuriates Ruggieri is the very nature of Ugolino's liaison with Gianetta. Ugolino notes that when he protected Gianetta from Ruggieri, she called "Pisa's liberator" her "rescuer." "Ruggieri then once more recognized Gherardesca, the man!"[8] Ugolino appropriates Gianetta on the basis of personal achievement as liberator of Pisa and individual character as a man, criteria that undercut conventional bases of authority in birth and station. In forcing Ruggieri to acknowledge his personal right to appropriate Gianetta in the private sphere, Ugolino challenges the Archbishop's authority, raising the storm of fury in his soul. "Here I was king!" Ugolino declares. "Here I was worshipped!"[9] As king in his own home, Ugolino infringes on the secular authority of the sovereign; worshipped by his progeny, he usurps the spiritual authority of the Church. As father who is worshipped in his home as king, Ugolino effectively declares his family's independence from the authority of Church and state, and as Pisa's top prelate, Ruggieri cannot countenance this.

---

[7] "[L]iebevoll und schüchtern sankst du in meine Arme. ... [Ruggieris] bleifarbichtes wässerichtes Angesicht tobte vom Sturm seiner Seele." (42)

[8] "[Ruggieri] wälzte seine adrichten Augen weit hervor; Tücke und Verderben lauschten nicht mehr im Schleier der Nacht! ... Da erkannte Ruggieri noch einmal Gherardesca, den Mann! ... [D]eine Wonnelippen nannten Pisas Befreier deinen Erretter." (43)

[9] "Hier war ich König! ... Hier war ich angebetet!" (42)

The play's most direct reference to the political struggle between Ugolino and Ruggieri appears in Act I. "Pisa groaned under the yoke of a tyrant," Francesco explains. "Gherardesca rose up and avenged her misery." Anselmo calls this act noble, and Francesco concurs. "But then Ruggieri, long secretly envious of him," Francesco continues, "persuaded him that the good of Pisa called for a master, and nobody had more of a right to Pisa's crown than Gherardesca. Gherardesca dared the bold step for which he will never forgive himself; and Gherardesca was ruined." Faced with the prospect of Ugolino's despotism, Ruggieri and the powerful houses of Pisa plotted against him, and "so Gherardesca fell."[10]

Ugolino aspired to rule Pisa not on the basis of corporative rank, but by virtue of his achievement as liberator of Pisa. Not as count, but as Pisa's liberator Ugolino once honored a prince (the brightest luminary in the corporative constellation) by seating him to his right at his table. Ugolino's title as count is scarcely mentioned in the play and amounts to little more than a concession to literary convention and historical accuracy. Ugolino's autocratic ambitions emanate from a sense of self-worth based not on birth and station, but on personal accomplishment.

Since they are not based on birth and station, Ugolino's ambitions are illegitimate by traditional standards. They alienate the "Gualandi, Sismondi, Lanfranchi" and the rest of what may be regarded as the aristocracy led by the Archbishop, who spurns and ridicules Ugolino's aspirations. By contrast, Ruggieri's status as prelate is highly profiled in the play. His stature within Pisa's aristocracy affords him a traditionally legitimate pretense to authority symbolized by the biretta he mockingly places on Anselmo's head.

Ugolino bases the legitimacy of his claim to absolute rule on the good of Pisa. "[Father] knows how to rule," Anselmo observes confidently. "Yes, and I can tell you that it is sweet to be ruled by Father," Gaddo agrees. "...[B]etween us, one is safest when one obeys him."[11] This suggests the social contract that characterized Enlightened absolut-

---

[10] "Pisa seufzte unter dem Joche eines Tyrannen. Gherardesca stand auf und rächte die Seufzende. ... Aber nun blies ihm Ruggieri, schon lange sein heimlicher Neider, den Gedanken ein, Pisas Wohl erfodre einen Beherrscher, niemand habe ein höheres Recht auf Pisas Diadem als Gherardesca. Gherardesca wagte den kühnen Schritt, den er sich nie verzeihen wird; und Gherardesca ward unglücklich. ... So fiel Gherardesca." (17-18)

[11] —"[Vater] versteht sich aufs Herrschen." —"Ja, und es ist süß, kann ich dir sagen, von unserm Vater beherrscht zu werden. ... Unter uns, man geht am sichersten, wenn man ihm gehorcht." (24)

ism and that lent itself so readily to the legitimizing metaphor of patriarchal sovereign (*Landesvater*): just as the autocratic family father protects and provides for his children in return for their absolute obedience, so the Enlightened despot rules for the commonweal in exchange for his subjects' complete subservience.

In broad strokes, Gerstenberg depicts Ugolino's history and fate in terms of the social dynamics underpinning eighteenth-century absolutism. With a new-found non-corporative sense of accomplishment and worth, Ugolino vies for power in order to extend the benevolent despotism of the intimate family circle into the public sphere. The family becomes an arena for testing and developing political models and agendas opposing the parochial interests of petty despotism in the public sphere. However, Ugolino is manipulated in a Machiavellian manner by Ruggieri, who uses him to play off the estates against each other and seize power himself.

But Ugolino is more than a mere pawn of history. As an historical actor, he is responsible for his own fate and for that of his children. When Anselmo praises him as a great man, Ugolino cuts him short. "No more! ... The author of your ruin, the disturber of your peace, the tyrant, the traitor is I!"[12] Ugolino assumes blame for his family's fate, but the problem is not public activity per se, since his role as Pisa's liberator appears heroic. Nor is it the patriarchal principle per se, which works well for Gaddo and Anselmo on the private level. Rather, the problem is Ugolino's idea of extending the patriarchal principle from the private family sphere to the public one.

This idea, cleverly suggested as it is, in Francesco's words, by "the emissary from hell [Ruggieri]," appears devilish.[13] The patriarchal principle, predicated in the private sphere on filial devotion, is corrupted when extended into the public sphere, where those in power use deceit and manipulation to get there. Ugolino's tragic flaw is misplaced confidence in the public power of private-sphere values such as personal merit and the loyalty of family and friends. Manipulated and betrayed not only by Ruggieri, but also by "all his friends and admirers," Ugolino is no longer able to protect his family, and this is the source of his rage and guilt.[14] In his failed attempt to rise both above his station (in aspiring

---

[12] "Nicht weiter! ... Der Urheber eures Verderbens, der Störer eurer Ruhe, der Herrschsüchtige, der Verräter, der bin ich!" (13)

[13] "...der Gesandte des Abgrundes, der, um sicherer zu verschlingen, im priesterlichen Mantel der Religion umherschleicht...." (17)

[14] Francesco tells Anselmo that "alle seine Freunde und Bewundrer" aban-

to be prince) and beyond it (in projecting private sphere values onto the public sphere), he has broken his end of the bargain implicit in the patriarchal principle: protection in return for unquestioning obedience.

In reaffirming the patriarchal ideal, the play projects a legitimizing metaphor for eighteenth-century absolutism. The concept of tyranny, vague in the play, does not suggest despotism per se, but rather its Machiavellian variant: despotic power for its own sake rather than for the good of all. The hate of tyrants — a popular theme at the time — does not imply democratic or even anti-authoritarian proclivities. Ugolino calls himself tyrant in connection with his failure to protect and provide for his children, not primarily because of his autocratic ambitions.

Nevertheless, the play carries a critical moment in implying that the absolutist state is not (as it purports to be) ruled by benevolent despots, but rather by self-aggrandizing autocrats such as Ruggieri. Although the story is set abroad and in the distant past, and although Gerstenberg carefully attributes it to somebody else (Dante), its appeal suggests that contemporaries viewed the problems it presents as not at all outlandish, but rather as consistent with their own experience: the patriarchal principle of benevolent autocracy appears at home in the private sphere, but not in public.

Anselmo's idealistic image of the intimate, exclusive family circle whole unto itself suggests the nature of this problem: the proclaimed ideal invokes the presence of a mother made absent by the machinations of public authority (Ruggieri). Anselmo naively expresses a sense of exclusive family identity that seems practically inescapable — consigned as it is to the tower — yet has grown questionable. At the same time, the threat of starvation in the tower places any definition of private-sphere identity that excludes public activity in doubt. The play's plot, imagery and historical references explore this problem: how viable is a non-corporative sense of identity excluding and excluded from contemporary arenas of public power?

Idyllic Nature

Perhaps the clearest articulation of non-corporative identities emerges in Act II, when Gaddo and Anselmo remember nature scenes near their father's villa. The bucolic terrain, potentiated by youthful imagination, allows Gerstenberg to explore alternatives to incarceration in the

doned Ugolino. (18)

tower. Freed from conflict with corporative authority, how might the emerging non-corporative strata interact?

Gaddo dreams that he is back home and has just eaten, and at first he believes it actually happened. Anselmo tries to persuade Gaddo that freedom is more important than eating. "What do I care about freedom!" Gaddo grumbles. "As long as I have something to eat!"[15] The operative relationship between the boys is competitive and adversarial as each claims authoritative knowledge of what is real and important.

Anselmo finally prevails by using his powers of empirical observation and aesthetic evocation to control and manipulate his brother in the name of freedom. First, he forces Gaddo to concede that he is not back home and has not eaten. Then he gets him to forget his unhappiness by appealing to his memories of nature scenery near Ugolino's villa. Anselmo's vision of parks, forests, and fields gradually overpowers Gaddo. When he focuses on particular birds and fish, Gaddo covers his mouth. "Don't speak about it anymore, Anselmo," he implores. "You've got me."[16]

Anselmo narrows the scope of his panoramic view until it encompasses only the silvery spring where the boys are bathing beneath a bank of flowers. By now, Gaddo is spell-bound by Anselmo's aesthetic evocation of nature. "Let me go!" he pleads, begging for permission to catch the eels Anselmo mentions. "Have I got you, rascal?" Anselmo gloats.[17]

Anselmo's silvery spring amid chirping birds and shady plants beneath a flowery cliff is typically idyllic. Enclosed by banks and vegetation, the idyll appears self-contained. Its elements are affixed within it. Father, mother, and all three brothers are mentioned or implied in connection with Ugolino's villa, evoking a time when the family circle was complete. Hovering motionless in time and space like the "eels swaying in the shade," the idyll triumphs over change, difference, and conflict.

Although Anselmo's appeal to idyllic nature imagery is avowedly liberating, his use of it is not. Anselmo's crystal trout streams, game birds, and "melting lamprey" evoke images of food, transforming his aesthetic subjects into the means to capture his starving brother. By affixing static details and spatial relations in a remembered context of idyllic nature, Anselmo weaves a web of family unity in and with which to captivate his brother, whose surrender ("You've got me!") and subsequent pleading ("Let me go!") reflect his entrapment. In structure and

---

[15] "Was geht mich Freiheit an! Hab ich doch zu essen!" (22)

[16] "Sprich nicht mehr davon, Anselmo. Du hast mich ganz." (23)

[17] —"Laß mich! laß mich!" ... —"Hab ich dich, Schalk?" (23)

function, Anselmo's vision of freedom near home and family in idyllic nature undermines its own liberating premise, replacing one prison with another.

Anselmo's manipulation of his brother suggests the egocentrism and competitive drive underlying even the most intimate relations among those on the margins of traditional society. The discourse between Anselmo and Gaddo is characterized by an empirical (and therefore self-oriented and divisive) appreciation of reality, a latent fear of conflict and change, and the manipulation of others to selfish ends. Behind the harmonious facade of the intimate family circle in idyllic nature lie conflicts and tensions that threaten to tear it apart.

The idyll's violent undercurrent emerges in a metaphor from the hunt: the swaying eels slip away faster "than the reed arrow from the gut string." In Dante, Ugolino dreams he is a wolf hunted by Ruggieri and his dogs. Gerstenberg adapts the theme of the hunt to his own purposes: the hunter becomes Anselmo, a member of the intimate family circle, and his prey becomes Gaddo, his own brother. The metaphor of the bow and arrow prefigures Anselmo's later personification of a tiger stalking the marten that he imagines Gaddo to be.

The boys' mother anxiously calls them, since Francesco had once almost drowned in the silvery spring. Paradoxically, this image of hidden menace in idyllic nature rounds out the family presence by introducing Gianetta and Francesco to the scene. At the same time, it destroys the idyll's timelessness by placing it in the context of history: at one point in time, the intimate family circle was threatened with destruction when Francesco almost drowned. The past refers to the present, when again in the course of events Gianetta is faced with the possibility of losing her eldest son, who has just escaped from the tower to face danger outside, and when Gianetta herself is threatened.

Anselmo again uses idyllic nature imagery to banish nature's threat while seducing his brother: the boys pick flowers and weave them into a wreath for their mother. Gaddo picks the flowers, while Anselmo weaves the wreath. However, they quarrel over what flowers should go into the wreath and who gets the reward (bestowal of the wreath by their mother). In the heat of the argument, they forget about their mother, who disappears from mention.

Anselmo seeks to stabilize the new order under the benevolent rule of his father. He imagines that Ugolino becomes ruler of Pisa and grants the boys property with livestock and forests. The boys again argue over who gets what, this time more violently. Anselmo forbids Gaddo from entering his forests, and when Gaddo insists, Anselmo grows irate.

The original discourse of family unity and harmony near Ugolino's villa culminates in violent conflict over power and property. As father replaces mother in the boys' discourse, they move from family intimacy into questions of property ownership. In providing for private property, the patriarchal principle initiates a struggle of all against all over ownership rights, undermining family intimacy.

Even though the quarrel ends on a conciliatory note, the reprieve is only temporary. Anselmo promises to give Gaddo his nests, deer, and forests, but his imaginary generosity fails to meet Gaddo's real need for food. In Act IV, Gaddo borrows a coin from Francesco and attempts to buy one of Anselmo's eggs. Marketplace values appear more real and effective than the values of family intimacy or aesthetic evocation.

Anselmo considers his brother's request for an egg a ploy to steal his property. He challenges Gaddo to a singing contest, then defends his eggs by stalking his brother with leading questions, finally closing quite literally for the kill. The idyll at the silvery spring, which expresses Anselmo's aspirations to freedom, leads to the violent imagery of predator and prey. Anselmo imagines himself a tiger stalked by hunters, Francesco calls Anselmo a lynx, and Gaddo is a martin stealing eggs. Returning to his senses, Anselmo pleads with heaven to protect him from "the enclosing claw," an allusion to the brutal violence in nature that he has just acted out.[18] Nature's terror emerges as the ideology of family intimacy gives way to competition among atomized individuals for power, property, and survival.

The Storm

The play's central image of violent nature, the storm, has a complex and contradictory character inversely complementing that of the tower. Insofar as the tower shelters and stimulates developing non-corporative values and relations in the private sphere, the storm threatens it with internal rupture and external buffeting. Conversely, insofar as the tower stifles and strangles non-corporative development, the storm represents the liberating potential of political struggle against corporative hegemony.

The storm has torn a hole in the tower near its peak, which Francesco widens enough to slip through. He plans to use the breach to rally Ugolino's remaining allies and free his family from the tower. By offering an opportunity to contest power in public outside, the storm opens the way to freedom.

---

[18] "Die umspannende Kralle." (51)

When Ugolino hears of the breach, he wonders whether he can use it to see into the street. "It would be a new, beautiful sight for me," he declares, "to see human beings, the image of God, outside these walls too; as little as those in Pisa deserve it of me."[19] Ugolino's vision of a Pisa full of human beings in the image of God lends substance to his sons' call for freedom. Since God is a concept of infinite authority and perfection, to the extent that Ugolino's sons partake of His image, they cannot be superior to each other. They are intrinsically equal among themselves and above or beyond any temporal hierarchy or authority. In the context of contemporary corporative society, with its rigid hierarchies based on birth and station, this is a profoundly subversive notion. Not only does it claim freedom from traditional corporative hierarchies for members of the intimate family circle, it would also emancipate those on the streets outside.

Ugolino hopes to liberate society at large merely by peering out from the tower. This implies an astonishing faith in the power of individual perception to change the world. Behind it lurks an aesthetic ideology of egoism: from the dominating vantage point of the tower peak, Ugolino would transform Pisans into amorphous human beings in a single image, all for the aesthetic pleasure of the solitary beholder. Ugolino's sons disappear from discourse, banished behind the adverbial adjunct "too." Ugolino's subversive vision of a Pisa populated by human beings is undermined by the very terms of its articulation. While the anticipated commanding view from the tower's peak would eliminate one tyranny, it would replace it with another by subsuming Pisa under Ugolino's own ego. The ambiguity of Ugolino's pronouncement that Pisans little deserve such a fate — which reflects his guilt concerning his tyrannical ambitions — suggests ambivalence towards his own emancipatory project.

Inspired by his sons' enthusiasm, Ugolino leaves to inspect what he now calls not just a breach, but an opening in the tower. "If only he doesn't plunge down onto the monster in the noble wrath of his heart," Francesco declares, "like the sublime bird who throws himself into the canyon where he saw a dragon."[20] Nature, it would seem, provides both the impetus and opportunity for a liberating battle between good

---

[19] "Es würde mir ein neuer, schöner Anblick sein, auch außer diesen Wänden Menschen, das Bild Gottes, zu erblicken; so wenig die in Pisa es um mich verdient haben." (15)

[20] "Wenn er sich nur nicht im edlen Grimm seines Herzens auf das Ungeheuer herabstürzt, gleich dem erhabnen Vogel, der sich ins Steintal wirft, wo er einen Drachen erblickte." (202)

and evil. The storm has breached the walls that prevent Ugolino from getting at his enemy. Outside the tower, he would become part of wild nature itself, a bird searching for prey over a canyon. Like an eagle, Ugolino would then instinctively prey on his natural enemy Ruggieri the dragon lurking in the canyon (or street) below. In Christian allegory, the struggle between Christ and Satan was often depicted in terms of a battle between an eagle and a dragon, the outcome of which signalled the millennial liberation of mankind in a Kingdom of Heaven on earth. Gerstenberg secularizes the allegory while preserving its emancipatory intent: the intimate circle in the private sphere is locked by nature in mortal combat with corporative forces in public, a conflict that promises to make the Gherardescas, in Francesco's words, "free, free as God created you."

Curiously, however, Francesco hopes that his father will *not* confront and destroy the Archbishop, even though this would mean his own liberation from prison. Anselmo knows why: Francesco himself wants the glory of liberating his father and brothers.[21] "No, no, my father," Francesco responds when Ugolino forbids his escape, "my presence is indispensable, and Francesco shall save you."[22] Behind a rhetoric of altruism, Francesco appears primarily concerned with his own role: longing for personal prestige, he rejects the prospect of a liberating confrontation between Ugolino and the Archbishop.

Ugolino's own reasons for rejecting an escape attempt reveal an even more pronounced retreat from an emancipatory struggle with corporative forces in public. Something changes when Ugolino actually looks through the opening in the tower. In a process of aesthetic apperception, he had hoped to sweep the streets below of Ruggieri's minions, replacing them with "human beings." Instead, Ugolino discovers that the opening actually entails unacceptable risks: the leap seems impossible, and spies lurk below. In what may be an early critique of the incipient aestheticism of his day, Gerstenberg suggests its powerlessness to effect hoped-for change.

Disappointed in his aesthetic expectations, Ugolino resigns himself to his fate. He recoils from the only alternative, practical measures leading to actual confrontation; he shuns the violent terrain of wild nature, since it leads to dangerous conflict in public. Instead, he accepts

---

[21] "Wie wird's des Übermütigen Herz aufschwellen, wenn unsere Mutter mit dem Finger hinzeigt, sprechend: 'Seht, dies ist mein Erstgeborner, der seinen Vater und seine beiden Brüder befreite!'" (16)

[22] "Nein, nein, mein Vater, meine Gegenwart ist unentbehrlich, und Francesco soll dich retten." (19)

and even welcomes incarceration in the private sphere as long as it shelters him from the dangerous storm of events outside.

Francesco responds differently. The storm spells two changes for him, each rife with emancipatory implications: it has ripped open the tower walls, and (as Francesco imagines) it has swept the streets of Ruggieri's agents, leaving them free for him to occupy at the head of an army of Ugolino's allies. However, Francesco's description of the storm's subversive portent suggests a hidden fear: the storm, he says, "threatens to tear the earth from its axis."[23] The storm's prospect of emancipation promises universal destruction. Far from undermining Ruggieri's power, the storm actually serves his purposes: its violence encourages Francesco's escape attempt by reassuring him that no spies are outside, and his escape, facilitated by the storm itself, turns into another way of torturing Ugolino when his son is symbolically returned to the tower in a coffin.

The public terrain of violent nature saps Francesco's energy when he reaches the streets. Instead of marshalling strength in preparation for a violent confrontation, he begins to lose strength and resolve. Reeling, he flees for the shelter of his mother's palace. There, he is blinded by fright at the first sign of confrontation with the Archbishop, his mother's death. When he revives, he is again overwhelmed by a poisonous potion. He awakens inside a coffin not knowing where he is. His father berates him for not using his fists to resist capture, while Anselmo mocks him for fleeing from danger outside to the seeming safety of the private sphere.

Ugolino is also blinded by adversity. Ruggieri's minions, he confesses, seized him "in the darkest of all nights ... so that I could not see around me" to seize Ruggieri "between my outstretched hands."[24] Ugolino even thanks the Archbishop for "removing the bear from his lair," for preventing him from defending home and family. Like Francesco, Ugolino not only fails to resist arrest, but appears blinded by fear at the very prospect of confrontation with the Archbishop.

Similarly, the confrontation with Gaddo that grows out of Anselmo's competitive discourse with him blocks his vision and saps his strength. Anselmo's eyes darken as he stalks his brother, and he emerges from delusion dizzy. Nature now appears in an alien and frightening "revolu-

---

[23] "In diesem Sturme, der die Erde aus ihren Angeln zu reißen droht? Wozu Kundschafter?" (18)

[24] "Daß deine Büttel mich unter der schwärzesten aller Nächte ... niederdrücken mußten, daß ich nicht um mich her schauen, ... dich nicht zwischen meine ausgestreckten Hände fassen ... konnte!" (9)

tion" (*im Kreise*), without corners or points of familiarity by which to orient oneself. Anselmo recoils from it in fear and loathing.

Ironically, their father finds Anselmo and Gaddo "together in this charming intimacy," suggesting his own blindness in the face of the internecine conflicts that undermine the myth of the intimate family circle. In the final Act, after killing Anselmo in a fit of rage, Ugolino laments that "my eyes are struck with blindness."[25] Confronted by external menace or internal conflict, the members of the intimate family circle lose vision and strength, fleeing in terror before adversity. Ugolino's commanding view from the tower, like Anselmo's bird's-eye view of nature terrain below, are powerful means of envisioning liberation. However, Ugolino, Anselmo, and Francesco are all ultimately blinded by the frightening course of events in the violent nature terrain both outside and inside the tower.

The promise of liberation through confrontation is revealed to be false. "The blind one revolted against the one who sees," Francesco tells his father upon his return. "I have been punished, my father."[26] In captivity, Francesco overhears Ruggieri's plan to board up the tower and let the Gherardescas starve, and he bemoans his escape attempt for saddling him with the responsibility of sharing this terrible knowledge. The storm itself forecasts the news: Ugolino contrasts the noises rescuers would make trying to break into the tower with what he does hear, the howling of winds past solid, unbroken surfaces and the patter of rain on them. Instead of tearing a liberating opening in the walls, the storm ultimately seals the Gherardescas' awful fate.

Nature's Terror

Paradoxically, once the opening is closed, nature's violence pierces the tower walls in full force, driving the inmates against each other in deadly confrontations. "The wolf is in me!" Anselmo cries as he starts to cannibalize his mother's body.[27] This sight overwhelms Ugolino. "Oh now shake, earth! now roar, storm winds! now whimper, nature! ... the hour of your giving birth is a great hour!"[28] In violating the natural

---

[25] "Doch meine Augen sind mit Blindheit geschlagen!" (64)

[26] "Der Blinde lehnte sich wider den Sehenden auf. Ich bin bestraft, mein Vater." (31)

[27] "Der Wolf ist in mir!" (58)

[28] "O nun beb, Erde! nun brüllt, Sturmwinde! nun wimmre, Natur! wimmre, Gebärerin! wimmre! wimmre! die Stunde deines Kreißens ist eine große

taboos underlying the intimate family circle, Anselmo precipitates a revolutionary rebirth (*Kreißen*) in nature that destroys the family. "You are not your mother's son, you monster!" Ugolino cries before murdering him.[29] Francesco's earlier warning against the storm that threatens to tear the earth from its axis now assumes its proper context: the violent storm of events and conflicts both inside and outside the private sphere is not a portent of freedom, but rather a menace to the family itself, not something to be hoped for, but feared and abhorred.

Full realization of his hopeless situation leads Ugolino to bewail it in a striking condemnation of individual isolation in the private sphere.

> I cannot protect myself from you; you abode of horror! no longer prison of your humiliation! tomb! tomb of Gherardesca's bones! ... all alone, my wife, my children gathered around me! still all alone! every sense full of their putrefaction! more terrible than alone![30]

Ugolino's self-centered lamentation expresses his very predicament. Although all three sons are still alive, Ugolino focuses on himself. The fate of his family affects him only insofar as the prospective smell of putrefying bodies around him reminds him of the horror of solitude. In dismissing his sons from mention, Ugolino displays an egoistic self-preoccupation, then recoils in horror from the isolation it implies.

Renouncing a private sphere that has become a house of horror, doomed by conflicts from without and within, Ugolino instead seeks a traditional source of solace: abandoning this life for the next. The analogies between Ugolino's suffering and Job's trials as well as Christ's passion are plain. "He called himself the one forsaken by God," Francesco says of him;[31] the three days and three nights of his tribulations are from the Bible, not Dante. Taking a cue from Anselmo, who repeatedly insists that hope lies in the beyond and dies singing a verse

---

[29] "Du bist deiner Mutter Sohn nicht, du Ungeheuer!" (59)

[30] "Ich kann mich deiner nicht erwehren; du Wohnhaus des Schreckens! nicht mehr Kerker deiner Erniedrigung! Gruft! Gruft der Gebeine Gherardescas! ... ganz einsam, mein Weib, meine Kinder rings um mich gesammelt! dennoch ganz einsam! jeder Sinn voll ihrer Verwesung! fürchterlicher als einsam!" (43-44)

[31] "Er nannte sich den von Gott Verlassenen." (55)

to this effect,[32] Ugolino concludes by raising his eyes to God and finds that "my torn soul is healed."[33]

The modern theme of inner rupture (*Zerrissenheit*) thereby finds one of its earliest expressions in German literature, curiously in the context of a traditional pronouncement. Ugolino repeats it in the play's last lines: "My torn soul is healed." This statement contains two distinct elements: the diagnosis of a malady (the torn soul) and its cure (healing by turning to the hereafter). Only the cure is traditional; the diagnosis is new. Unlike the Biblical Job, whose troubles are visited upon him by unfathomable otherworldly forces that test his faith, Ugolino's woes stem from conflict with the Archbishop and within his own family, both of this world, and both internalized within Ugolino himself.

Internalization of the conflict is its essence. Although surrounded by his dead family slain by a tyrant who rules his homeland, Ugolino remains primarily concerned with himself. In his final soliloquy, he refers to his family and to Ruggieri only in terms of how they affect his decision whether or not to commit suicide. "How my fellow Pisan consigned to damnation [Ruggieri] would show his teeth grinning!" he intones bitterly before continuing on a note of self-pity: "Forgive me! ... Haven't my poor innocent children already fallen?"[34] These two poles of his existence — the Archbishop and his family — exist primarily not for themselves, but rather for and within Ugolino. Ruggieri, his former friend whom he says he could have loved, with whom he identifies as tyrant, traitor, and fellow consignee to damnation, becomes for Ugolino both an adversary and alter ego. Ugolino's family members are what Francesco calls branches from the trunk of an oak, or what Ugolino calls his own "members" (*Glieder*), in either case part and parcel of Ugolino himself. Even the means whereby the limbs fall from the torso are implemented by Ugolino himself: he writes Gianetta the poisoned letter that kills her and that entices Francesco into a deadly ambush, and he kills Anselmo outright. Ugolino's self-pity illustrates both the egoistic kernel of his non-corporative identity and its destructive — and ultimately self-destructive — character.

Paralyzed by fear of conflict with public authority, Ugolino faces a quandary: in order to survive, he must escape from the tower and contest Ruggieri's authority in public; his non-corporative values, aspirations, and history as liberator of Pisa all impel him to do so. Yet he

---

[32] "Jenseits ist die Aussicht;" (62) "Ist ... [n]icht im Tale des Todes Wonnegesang?" (65)

[33] "Meine zerrissene Seele ist geheilt." (65)

[34] "Wie würde der mitverdammte Pisaner die Zähne blöcken! ... [V]ergib mir! ... Sind nicht meine armen unschuldigen Kinder gefallen?" (66)

cannot surmount his fear of conflict, which keeps him incarcerated inside the tower and spells his doom. This dilemma is reflected in Ugolino's torn soul, linking the modern problem of inner rupture with the emergence of a non-corporative social sector in Germany in conflict with traditional society. In 1768, the problem could still be resolved by turning to traditional religious solutions; by 1815, this was no longer possible. In that year, Gerstenberg ended his second version of the play without referring to the healing power of the hereafter. Instead, the curtain falls as Ugolino is about to commit suicide.

Gerstenberg's violent nature imagery expresses the apparent disaster that he finds the emergence of non-corporative identities to be. The storm outside seems to offer the opportunity of liberation, but when Francesco dares to take advantage of it, he lives to regret it. Ruggieri's reign outside the tower is associated with the storm, with nature; challenging it amounts to *hubris* and is violently punished. Corporative authority is obliquely affirmed as the victims, blaming themselves, forgive the Archbishop and, abandoning their aspirations, return to traditional values.

If conflict with the Archbishop stems from the very nature of the Gherardescas, and if this conflict is ultimately self-defeating, then non-corporative aspirations that lead to the conflict ultimately emerge as the source of the problem. The language of nature expresses the conflicts and contradictions that could emerge from the unencumbered pursuit of non-corporative identities. As an idyll, nature becomes a means to an end, a tool of domination and exploitation. As a violent menace, nature represents the reverse side of the same coin — the antagonisms and conflicts brewing beneath the placid surface of family harmony. The historical project of the Gherardescas — their search for a new, non--corporative sense of identity free of conflict — ends in abject failure as the original vision of family intimacy is transformed into a nightmare in which the strong prey on the weak like animals in the wild. In the process of re-membering itself in a past Golden Age of unity and harmony with nature, the intimate family circle consumes its own utopian premise. Freed from the strictures of corporative society, the isolated strata would self-destruct.

After the Lisbon earthquake of 1755, a new view of nature developed in Germany designed to appeal to the concrete experience of the new bourgeoisie. Gerstenberg's nature imagery deepens the language of literature into a critical commentary on a changing world. The problem of individual isolation on the margins of corporative society was further defined by what is often considered the centerpiece of Sturm und Drang literature: Goethe's *Werther*.

4

Nature and Self in Goethe's *Werther*

JOHANN WOLFGANG GOETHE'S *Die Leiden des jungen Werther* catapulted its young author to literary fame across Europe. Within a year of its publication in 1774, *Werther* was reprinted. The novel was so popular that Goethe even made money on it (unusual for the time). The first French translation appeared in 1776, followed by an English translation in 1779 and Italian and Russian translations in 1781. Napoleon carried *Werther* with him in Egypt and asked to interview its author in 1808. A Werther cult mushroomed, Werther dress was widely copied, and the Werther mood of introspective melancholy was sometimes taken to the point of suicide.

The work's appeal to suicide led to controversy. Within a few months of *Werther*'s appearance, Christoph Friedrich Nicolai parodied it in his *Die Freuden des jungen Werther*, only the first of many writings inspired by the troubling and purportedly troublesome work, which was eventually banned in Saxony and Denmark. Contemporary commentators on Werther fell into three camps: those like Johann Heinrich Merck who defended its life-like character portraiture; those like Gotthold Ephraim Lessing who admired its poetic beauty, but argued that it failed to morally educate its audience; and those like Melchior Goeze for whom it blasphemed by portraying the ultimate sin of suicide in a sympathetic light.[1]

Although the debate focused on suicide, its subtext was the ongoing controversy over the nature of reality and the role of art in it. For Goethe and his adherents, reality was defined in terms of concrete individual

---

[1] For a thorough discussion of *Werther's* contemporary reception, see Horst Flaschka, *Goethe's Werther* (Munich: Fink, 1987), 239-288.

experience, and art was designed to give it natural expression. For much of the Enlightenment camp as well as proponents of religious orthodoxy, reality was a predefined order of higher truths ultimately grounded in God, and art was supposed to illuminate it or instruct an audience on how to live up to its moral precepts. *Werther*'s popularity not only suggests that ever larger audiences were embracing individual experience rather than abstract principles as the measure of reality, but that Werther's particular experience in Goethe's novel captured the imagination of much of the reading public itself.

What was it about Goethe's novel that appealed to contemporary audiences? Werther's persistent evocation of nature in pursuing his own sense of identity seems ambivalent: while liberating him from stultifying social constraints, it gradually isolates and destroys him. What appears dysfunctional in the novel is not so much the social or moral fabric of the corporative order as Werther's marginal role within it. There is never any serious challenge to the social order, only the question of what to do with its misfits, including the murderous farmhand, the scribe driven mad by frustrated passion, and others who mirror Werther's situation. The novel offers a prognosis on dealing with marginal identities and aspirations in a world in which they have no place.

Apparently, contemporary audiences found much truth in the negativity of the prognosis, and this may be why it caused so much concern. There is a striking connection between Werther's professed pursuit of personal growth and his gradual self-destruction. As the idyllic nature imagery associated with Werther's aspirations gradually turns violent, Werther loses his ability to cope with a changing world. What does Werther's experience of violent nature in the work say about the contemporary experience of social change? Before turning to this question, I shall briefly discuss the social significance of the rise of aesthetics in the eighteenth century and the problem of nature it posed for Goethe.

Aesthetics and Metaphysics

In his influential study *Die Theorie des Romans* (1920), Georg Lukács describes the late eighteenth-century novel as a discourse on the illusion that individual identity can supplant a lost sense of traditional community.[2] The traditional ties of corporative society and their ideo-

---

[2] Georg Lukács, *Die Theorie des Romans* (Darmstadt, Neuwied: Luchterhand, 1979), 98-103. Peter Uwe Hohendahl develops a related argument in "Bürgerlichkeit und Bürgertum als Problem der Literatursoziologie," *German*

logical underpinnings in metaphysics were giving way to nascent capitalist relations and values. Art lost its traditional function of replicating and reproducing social ties and roles. With the collapse of the traditional order, art was freed of the metaphysical illusion of a seamless totality. In measuring individual experience, aesthetics instead could reveal ways in which artificial totalities are constructed.

However, aesthetics made itself into a new ideology by hypostatizing new seamless realities based on personal subjectivity. Not only did aesthetics claim autonomy from social relations, according to Lukács it initiated "a raping and wishing to destroy the essence of everything lying outside the realm of art, an attempt to forget that art ... has as the condition of its existence and coming to consciousness the collapse and inadequacy of the [traditional] world." Lukács suggests that eighteenth-century writers developed a new aesthetic ideology designed not only to supplant a lost nexus of corporative identity, but also to repress the changing social relations that produced it. "A new, paradoxical Greece has arisen," he concludes, "aesthetics have again become metaphysics."[3]

Goethe's *Werther* deals with the problem of aestheticism Lukács describes. As he confesses in *Dichtung und Wahrheit*, Goethe used the process of writing *Werther* to deal in his own life with some of Werther's problems, specifically a sense of alienation from others.[4] Elsewhere, he states that he used aesthetics to escape an uncontrollable demonic force in nature and society that frightened yet fascinated him.[5] Can *Werther* be viewed as an aesthetic process of compensating for the loss of corporative ties by repressing the social processes behind it?

Goethe's *Werther* draws on the tradition of eighteenth-century epistolary novels popularized by Samuel Richardson. Goethe's contribution to the genre was to eliminate a formal letter exchange while buttressing the fiction of a real-life basis to the story with expanded editorial commentary. This fiction has two effects. First, it gives an aura of naturalism to Werther's letters by distancing the author from the work

---

Quarterly 61 (1988), 264-283.

[3] "...ein Vergewaltigen und ein Vernichtenwollen der Wesenheit von allem, was außerhalb des Bereichs der Kunst liegt, ein Versuch zu vergessen, daß die Kunst ... das Auseinanderfallen und das Nichtausreichen der Welt zur Voraussetzung ihrer Existenz und ihres Bewußtwerdens hat. ... Es ist ein neues, paradoxes Griechentum entstanden, die Ästhetik ist wieder zur Metaphysik geworden." Lukács, *Theorie des Romans*, 30.

[4] Johann Wolfgang Goethe, *Dichtung und Wahrheit*, ed. Trunz, IX, 540-541.

[5] Goethe, *Dichtung und Wahrheit*, ed. Trunz, X, 175-177.

through the fictive editorial voice. The editor has presumably carefully collected whatever he could find on Werther's history, and he lets the compendium of documents speak for itself by arranging it in chronological order. In various footnotes, he suggests a real historical basis of events described (for instance, by claiming to have changed names found in the original).

The form of Goethe's novel creates the fiction that behind Werther's tale are real-life characters with distinct voices or identities. Each is separated and alienated from the reader and other characters by Werther's letters and the editor's perspective. The tendency to draw analogies from Werther to real historical figures (such as Karl Wilhelm Jerusalem, Johann Christian Kestner, Charlotte Buff, Maximiliane La Roche, Goethe himself) testifies both to the success of this aesthetic technique and to a desire to overcome its latent alienation. It presumes a world in which individuals with distinct identities are isolated from one another by fragmentary perspective.

Second, the editor implies that there is more to the story than he presents in the form of documents not found (notably Wilhelm's letters to Werther). While what Wilhelm may have written is occasionally apparent from Werther's replies, it is up to the reader to reconstruct missing segments in the correspondence. This technique gives the reader a voice in telling Werther's story.

However, Werther's one-sided correspondence reduces the primary perspective of the tale to Werther's own. The reader usually has little choice but to interpret conversations, events, and characters in the story from Werther's viewpoint. This technique leads the reader to empathize or even identify with Werther and his judgments. In his opening remarks, the editor states the aesthetic purpose of this focus on Werther's viewpoint in the telling form of a demand: "You cannot deny his spirit and his character your admiration and love, his fate your tears."[6] It is difficult to overlook the manipulative intent of this statement, suggesting that of the literary form itself.

The form of the novel suggests a fragmented reality in which the author, the editor, Wilhelm as recipient of Werther's letters and inferred writer of his own, Werther himself, each character he encounters, and the reader all have a distinct voice or identity of his or her own. There

---

[6] "Ihr könnt seinem Geist und seinem Charakter eure Bewunderung und Liebe, seinem Schicksale eure Tränen nicht versagen." Johann Wolfgang Goethe, *Die Leiden des jungen Werther* (Frankfurt: Insel, 1974), 7. Since all references to Goethe's *Werther* are from this edition, letters are indicated only by date, editorial comments only by page number following original text in the footnote.

is little coherence between or among the articulations of each. They are separated by the fragmentary character of letters and editorial references. This suggests that a primary issue in the novel is fragmentation itself, or individual identity cut off from a common context.

The problem of individual isolation is presented in a context of manipulation. "And you good soul," the editor intones, "who feel the same impulse as he, take comfort from his suffering, and let the book be your friend if due to fate or your own fault you can find no closer one."[7] The reader is presumed to have no better friend than a book and to share Werther's problem of isolation. In this context, "let the book be your friend" is an almost programmatic call for aesthetics to replace a lost sense of communication with others.

The form of the novel ties the central problem of fragmented perspective to related problems of individual isolation and self-interest. It insinuates that aesthetics can replace a nexus of lost ties, becoming what Lukács terms a new metaphysics. Behind this ideology, however, are the changing realities it is predicated on: the traditional roles and relations of corporative society give way to atomized individuals defining the world from their own particular perspectives and acting according to their own particular interests. While the form of *Werther* seems designed to establish a new aesthetic ideology, its subtext is a discourse on these changes.

The structure of Werther's letters highlights his problem of isolation. As he ruefully acknowledges on May 27, Werther's primary form of discourse has three structural elements: rapture, comparison, and declamation.[8] Werther begins many letters with rapturous emotion, then explicates his feelings metaphorically, and finally draws from them conclusions for humanity in general. On May 12, for instance, when he describes the enclosed spring, he begins by gushing about his marvelous sense of fantasy, then uses Biblical lore to illustrate it, and finally asserts that any visitor to the spring must equally share his "patriarchal ideal."

Werther acknowledges this kind of discourse as a problem. When he falls into it, he forgets to finish telling about two children he sketched. His self-absorption excludes others (in this case, the children) from discourse by preventing him from finishing the story. "I am content and happy," he declares after his first meeting with Lotte, "and therefore not

---

[7] "Und du gute Seele, die du eben den Drang fühlst wie er, schöpfe Trost aus seinem Leiden, und laß das Büchlein deinen Freund sein, wenn du aus Geschick oder eigener Schuld keinen nähern finden kannst." (7)

[8] "Ich bin, wie ich sehe, in Verzückung, Gleichnisse und Deklamation verfallen," Werther ruefully acknowledges in his letter of May 27.

a good story writer."⁹ This in turn interferes with his communication. "If I continue in this way," he admits after going on at length about his pleasure at meeting Lotte, "you will be no wiser at the end than at the beginning."¹⁰ Werther's usual self-oriented discourse impedes rather than enhances communication, rendering him incoherent.

Apparently at Wilhelm's urging, Werther undertakes a second kind of language, the recounting of a related sequence of events (what he calls story-telling). However, this kind of language does not come easily to him. For Werther, the historical form of discussion entails an empirical description of observed or experienced events rather than (or in addition to) his own inner feelings. It implies a world out there independent of Werther's own subjectivity, a difference difficult for Werther to articulate.

In the course of describing it, Werther often banishes it, displacing it with his own subjectivity. For instance, after describing the young woman he takes to the dance, Werther calls her unimportant, dismissing her from mention. By the end of his detailed account of his first meeting with Lotte, he writes that "the whole world is losing itself around me."¹¹ All that remains is Klopstock's aesthetic deification in Lotte's eyes.

Although Werther succeeds in relating the series of events that befall him, he becomes his story's focal point, the nexus connecting the web of told events, which vanish behind his own ego. Like his declamatory mode of language, Werther's story-telling initially acknowledges an other world beyond himself, only to eventually exclude it from mention. This suggests a conflict built into the very structure of Werther's letters between his own individual subjectivity and his experience of human relationships and interaction with the world outside. Two worlds in conflict emerge: the outside world of everyday life, and Werther's own inner aesthetic world of self-experience. Werther's project — and predicament — is to exclude the outside world by subsuming it under his own ego.

---

[9] "Ich bin vergnügt und glücklich, und also kein guter Historienschreiber." (June 16)

[10] "Wenn ich so fortfahre, wirst du am Ende so klug sein wie am Anfange." (June 16)

[11] "...die ganze Welt verliert sich um mich her." (June 19)

Werther's Isolation

How does this conflict with the outside world emerge, and how does Werther cope with it? Werther's first letter opens with a clear differentiation between a here and now and a past somewhere else. "How glad I am to be gone!"[12] Werther intones.

> Weren't my other relationships sought out by fate to frighten a heart like mine? Poor Leonore! ... And still — am I totally innocent? Didn't I nourish her feelings? ... didn't I — Oh what right does a person have to complain about himself! I want to ... improve myself, I won't belabor the little bit of misfortune that fate presents us with...; I will enjoy the present, and bygones shall be bygones for me.[13]

Werther briefly considers accepting responsibility for exploiting Leonore's passion for his own amusement, only to dismiss this notion on principle. He resolves not to let the "little bit of misfortune that fate presents us with" prevent him from enjoying himself now. The egoistic nature of the problem suggests an equally egoistic solution: avoiding troublesome relations with others altogether. While the past in the world out there is associated with annoying social ties and responsibilities, the present right here suggests a preferred world of solitude.

Of course, Werther's solitude is figurative. He is on a mission to recover part of an inheritance for his mother from a recalcitrant aunt. He uses this worldly business to further illustrate his dislike of the world, finding that "misunderstandings and idleness may produce more disputes in the world than cunning and malevolence."[14] Problems arise due to misunderstanding and alienation among Werther's social peers.

---

[12] "Wie froh bin ich, daß ich weg bin!" (May 4)

[13] "Waren nicht meine übrigen Verbindungen recht ausgesucht vom Schicksal, um ein Herz wie das meine zu ängstigen? Die arme Leonore! ... Und doch — bin ich ganz unschuldig? Hab' ich nicht ihre Empfindungen genährt? ... hab' ich nicht — O was ist der Mensch, daß er über sich klagen darf! Ich will ... mich bessern, will nicht mehr ein bißchen Übel, das uns das Schicksal vorlegt, wiederkäuen...; ich will das Gegenwärtige genießen, und das Vergangene soll mir vergangen sein." (May 4)

[14] "Und ich habe, mein Lieber, wieder bei diesem kleinen Geschäft gefunden, daß Mißverständnisse und Trägheit vielleicht mehr Irrungen in der Welt machen als List und Bosheit." (May 4)

Since Werther freely discusses social stratification in his letters, it quickly becomes apparent to which social sector he belongs. Werther travels in circles that include Lotte, whose father is a state functionary and whose fiance Albert obtains a position in the state apparatus. A physician visits Lotte's home informally enough to observe Werther playing with the children. His friend Wilhelm is a scholar, and together with Lotte he visits a vicar. He takes employment from a minister of state and works under a state emissary at a foreign court. Werther belongs to the state bureaucracy, and he associates socially with professionals. Both groups form part of the new bourgeoisie in Germany.

As part of the new bourgeoisie, Werther finds himself isolated from other social sectors. "People of some status," he observes, "will always keep themselves at a cold distance from the common people."[15] Although Werther fraternizes with a farmhand and helps a servant girl at the spring, he maintains his social distance. "I well know," he says, "that we are not and cannot be equal; but I maintain that whoever believes he must distance himself from the so-called riffraff in order to preserve respect is just as reproachable as a coward who hides from his enemy because he fears defeat."[16] Werther not only acknowledges deep divisions among the social strata, he explicitly affirms them. Moreover, by projecting the common people as the enemies of his own peers, Werther suggests a latent struggle between privileged and deprived sectors. His own fraternization with the enemy seems rooted more in the secure knowledge of social superiority than in any desire for social integration. Despite his willingness to chat with them and even to identify with their passions, Werther's condescending remarks about them reinforce his distance from them.

Werther's estrangement from the laboring sector is mirrored in his relations with the aristocracy. In working for the emissary at court, he fraternizes with aristocrats and, in a fateful blunder, overstays his welcome at Count von C.'s table. Although he apologizes to the Count, the scandal spreads, and Werther is chided by those at court for deeming himself above his condition. This faux pas helps destroy his career at court, affirming the deep divisions that separate the aristocracy from the new bourgeoisie.

---

[15] "Leute von einigem Stande werden sich immer in kalter Entfernung vom gemeinen Volke halten." (May 15)

[16] "Ich weiß wohl, daß wir nicht gleich sind, noch sein können; aber ich halte dafür, daß der, der nötig zu haben glaubt, vom sogenannten Pöbel sich zu entfernen, um den Respekt zu erhalten, ebenso tadelhaft ist als ein Feiger, der sich vor seinem Feinde verbirgt, weil er zu unterliegen fürchtet." (May 15)

For his part, Werther's derision of the aristocracy suggests resentment of its privileges. According to Werther, Fräulein von B.'s aunt faces "in her old age a lack of everything, no substantial fortune, no intellect, and no support ... other than the series of her ancestors, no protection other than the status in which she fortifies herself, and no other pleasure than to gaze from her heights across bourgeois heads."[17] Such remarks suggest that the aristocracy has lost any redeeming social value. It is outdated (Baron F.'s wardrobe, for instance, dates from the coronation of Emperor Franz I, or the 1740s) and lacks in the wealth and intellect or knowledge that alone confer status and social usefulness in new-bourgeois circles. Instead, the nobility draws on the empty formalities of birth and station in looking askance at non-aristocrats, and Werther feels outraged when Fräulein von B. tells him that her aunt severely chastised her for associating with him after his faux pas at court.

Despite sharply criticizing the aristocracy, Werther reluctantly yet firmly endorses the corporative conventions behind aristocratic privilege. "What bothers me the most," he complains,

> are the annoying civil conventions. Of course, I know as well as anyone else how necessary the difference among the estates is, how many advantages it provides me myself; the only thing is that it should not stand in my way right where I could still enjoy a little gladness, a glimmer of happiness on this earth.[18]

Werther's rationale is revealing: self-interest. To the extent that social differences provide Werther with advantages, it is plain to him how necessary they are. Only when they stymie his own pursuit of happiness does Werther condemn them. The traditional social ideal of corporative elements harmonizing in a well-tuned hierarchy contrasts sharply with this ethic of individual self-interest.

However, the obstacles of corporative privilege are only part of Werther's disaffection with the world outside. Werther reserves much of

---

[17] "...daß die liebe Tante in ihrem Alter Mangel von allem, kein anständiges Vermögen, keinen Geist und keine Stütze [hat] ... als die Reihe ihrer Vorfahren, keinen Schirm als den Stand, in den sie sich verpalisadiert, und kein Ergetzen, als von ihrem Stockwerk herab über die bürgerlichen Häupter wegzusehen." (December 24)

[18] "Was mich am meisten neckt, sind die fatalen bürgerlichen Verhältnisse. Zwar weiß ich so gut als einer, wie nötig der Unterschied der Stände ist, wie viel Vorteile er mir selbst verschafft: nur soll er mir nicht eben gerade im Wege stehen, wo ich noch ein wenig Freude, einen Schimmer Glück auf dieser Erde genießen könnte." (December 24)

his invective for his own social peers. He derides the young student V. for thinking he knows more than others and refuses to consort with him, although he congratulates himself on his own artistic talent and knowledge of Greek. With rare exceptions (Lotte and her father, the Vicar of St.), Werther finds his peers intolerable. The emissary for whom he works is a pedantic fool for criticizing his work, and the rest of his peers at court envy him and take advantage of his faux pas to gain a competitive advantage over him. He derides Albert for paying more attention to his career than to his bride Lotte.

Werther spurns the competition and careerism of his peers, focusing instead on his own inner self. In rejecting the work ethic and materialism of the new bourgeoisie, Werther resigns himself to the fate of alienation from his peers. When he forgets himself, he can still enjoy their company, "only it cannot [then suddenly] occur to me that so many other powers still rest within me."[19] At the heart of Werther's critique of his peers is an obsession with his own inner powers, egoistic predilection with his own potential.

Beginning with Leonore and his other relationships, Werther chooses to forsake troubling social ties and responsibilities. His own social sector's mundane concerns alienate Werther, while social differences thwart any real fraternization with his social inferiors and superiors. Werther is caught in a world of competition and careerism among his peers and conflict and confrontation among the social strata. His solution is to focus on himself. "I return within myself," he declares, "and find a world!"[20]

Nature's Promise

Werther's alternative world within finds expression in nature. "The city itself is unpleasant," Werther writes in his first letter, "by contrast all around [there is] an unspeakable beauty of nature." Nature's beauty is introduced as an alternative to an unpleasant world of social relations; its "solitude is an exquisite balsam for my heart in this region of paradise."[21] Since language is a social practice, and since Werther chooses

---

[19] "Wenn ich mich manchmal vergesse ... nur muß mir nicht einfallen, daß noch so viele andere Kräfte in mir ruhen." (May 17)

[20] "Ich kehre in mich selbst zurück, und finde eine Welt!" (May 22)

[21] "...die Einsamkeit ist meinem Herzen köstlicher Balsam in dieser paradiesischen Gegend. ... Die Stadt selbst ist unangenehm, dagegen ringsumher eine unaussprechliche Schönheit der Natur." (May 4)

to avoid social interaction in favor of solitude in nature, it follows that nature's beauty is unspeakable. It can only be experienced, not communicated. It presents a promise of fulfillment beyond the limits of extant social practice. Nature, aestheticized as myth (paradise), restores the isolated individual to wholeness by excluding social interaction.

It does so by transforming solitude into interaction with all of nature. "Every tree, every bush is a bouquet of blossoms, and one wishes to become a May bug in order to float around in the sea of pleasant smells and find all one's nourishment therein."[22] Nature is a sea of sensations from a plethora of sources that nourish each other. In becoming a May bug, Werther would join a self-contained communion of nature's elements with each other. The wholeness of nature compensates for Werther's abandoned ties to the world.

Nature's beauty inspired Count von M. to have a garden built nearby. "The garden is simple," Werther notes, "and one feels as soon as one enters that it was planned not by a scientific gardener, but by a feeling heart that wanted to enjoy itself here."[23] Werther vows to acquire the garden and look after its caretaker.

Designed to reflect its creator's own subjectivity, the garden subordinates nature to individual self-reflection. Werther's favorite spot in the garden is a small alcove, an enclosed space offering both a sense of security in isolation and a view of the valley below from the perspective of ownership and domination. At the same time, Werther's aesthetic appreciation of the garden leads to its material appropriation. Count von M., the aristocrat who owned the garden property (and presumably much of the surrounding terrain) is dead. Werther would use the financial power of the new bourgeoisie to purchase property formerly owned by an aristocracy in demise while assuming the traditional corporative duty of assuring the caretaker's livelihood. The aestheticization of nature in compensation for social alienation transforms nature into both a commodity and a mirror of the isolated individual, instances of the very alienation it is designed to overcome. At the same time, it is associated with the power to acquire property and assume the formality of corporative responsibilities in an era of corporative decline. The solitude that

---

[22] "Jeder Baum, jede Hecke ist ein Strauß von Blüten, und man möchte zum Maienkäfer werden, um in dem Meer von Wohlgerüchen herumschweben und alle seine Nahrung darin finden zu können." (May 4)

[23] "Der Garten ist einfach, und man fühlt gleich bei dem Eintritte, daß nicht ein wissenschaftlicher Gärtner, sondern ein fühlendes Herz den Plan gezeichnet, das seiner selbst hier genießen wollte." (May 4)

Werther cultivates in nature comments on changing social relations in late eighteenth-century Germany.

Where does this discussion lead? Werther develops it in his letter of May 10 in describing how nature heightens the self-absorption of the solitary soul:

> When the dear valley mists around me, and the sun up high rests on the surface of the impenetrable darkness of my forest, and only single rays steal into the inner sanctum, I then lie in the high grass by the falling brook and closer to the ground a thousand various blades of grass become noticeable to me; when I feel the swarming of the tiny world between the blades, the countless unfathomable figures of worms and flies closer to my heart, and feel the presence of the Almighty, who created us in His image, the swaying of the All-Loving One who carries and preserves us floating in eternal bliss; my friend! when it then grows dark around my eyes, and the world around me and the sky rest completely in my soul like the figure of a lover — then I often long and think: oh if you could express all this in return, if you could breathe onto paper what lives so fully, so warmly within you, so that it would become the mirror of your soul, as your soul is the mirror of eternal God! — My friend — But I perish over this, I succumb to the power of the glory of these appearances.[24]

The suggestion of nearby heights framing the valley with trees surrounding and shading a grassy area by a rushing brook indicates a traditional nature idyll (*locus amoenus*). Werther links this static nature imagery to

---

[24] "Wenn das liebe Tal um mich dampft, und die hohe Sonne an der Oberfläche der undurchdringlichen Finsternis meines Waldes ruht, und nur einzelne Strahlen sich in das innere Heiligtum stehlen, ich dann im hohen Grase am fallenden Bache liege und näher an der Erde tausend mannigfaltige Gräschen mir merkwürdig werden; wenn ich das Wimmeln der kleinen Welt zwischen Halmen, die unzähligen, unergründlichen Gestalten der Würmchen, der Mückchen näher an meinem Herzen fühle, und fühle die Gegenwart des Allmächtigen, der uns nach seinem Bilde schuf, das Wehen des All-liebenden, der uns in ewiger Wonne schwebend trägt und erhält; mein Freund! wenn's dann um meine Augen dämmert, und die Welt um mich her und der Himmel ganz in meiner Seele ruhn wie die Gestalt einer Geliebten — dann sehne ich mich oft und denke: ach könntest du das wieder ausdrücken, könntest du dem Papiere das einhauchen, was so voll, so warm in dir lebt, daß es würde der Spiegel deiner Seele, wie deine Seele ist der Spiegel des unendlichen Gottes! — Mein Freund — Aber ich gehe darüber zugrunde, ich erliege unter der Gewalt der Herrlichkeit dieser Erscheinungen." (May 10)

another ancient literary tradition, the cosmic vision of a "great chain of being." His references to the microcosmic worm in Friedrich Gottlieb Klopstock's influential ode "Die Frühlingsfeier" (1759) and to the "green myriads in the peopled grass" in Alexander Pope's *Essay on Man* (1736) affirm the vision of a harmonious hierarchy in nature rising from its humblest creatures through man to God.

Basil Willey has aptly called such imagery "cosmic Toryism."[25] In Pope's articulation of the great chain of being, each species is "alike essential to th'amazing whole," a precept with an explicit social corollary:

> Order is Heav'n's first law; and this confest,
> Some are, and must be, greater than the rest,
> More rich, more wise;...
>
> More pow'rful each as needful to the rest,
> And in proportion as it blesses, blest;
>
> Draw to one point and to one centre bring
> Beast, man, or angel, servant, lord, or king.

For Pope, "th'according music of a well-mix'd state" is part of "the world's great harmony," or the great chain of being. Each social sector has its own niche needful to the rest in the corporative hierarchy. "The bliss of Man," Pope concludes, is to accept "what his nature and his state can bear."[26] Since the corporative hierarchy is natural, striving beyond one's born state in life is correspondingly unnatural. Pope's famous maxim, "Whatever is, is right," projects a static, stratified, and hierarchical corporative order as a social ideal.

In reiterating Pope's cosmic vision, Werther implicitly cites the social ideal at its core. Pope's natural hierarchy of beast, man, and angel (or Werther's insect, man, and God) connotes his parallel social hierarchy of servant, lord, or king (Werther's differences among the estates). Werther's idyllic nature expresses a corporative ideal of harmonious social hierarchy.

---

[25] "Eighteenth-century optimism ... was in essence an apologia for the status quo." Basil Willey, *The Eighteenth-Century Background* (Boston: Beacon Press, 1961), 48.

[26] Pope, 37-38 (Ep. IV, lines 49-51); 34 (Ep. III, lines 293-302); 10 (Ep. I, lines 189-192).

However, a syntactic tension between Werther's "when" and "then" clauses strikes a discordant note in this harmony of nature's elements. Werther's nature description is syntactically structured as follows:

> When the dear valley mists around me..., I then lie in the high grass on the falling brook...; when I feel the swarming...; ...when it then grows dark around my eyes... — then I often long...[27]

The "when" clauses embrace Werther's cosmic vision of nature and a concomitant corporative ideal of changeless harmony. However, they also hold him prone, trapped, and hostage to the entrancing imagery of the surrounding valley, the impenetrable dark of forest, the high grass, the unfathomable figures of nature, and the embrace of God's hand. Although sheltered and nurtured by this vision of cosmic harmony, Werther linguistically strives to break its bonds. Each "when" clause formally reaches beyond itself toward the ultimate "then" clause that expresses his longing to sketch all that he sees and feels. The entire passage strives beyond Werther's cosmic vision, supplanting it with his desire for artistic expression. Artistic realization of the nature idyll would threaten its static self-containment by introducing processes of communication and social interaction characteristic of the city. It would reverse the order of things, enabling the individual subject to take control of his environment instead of lying under its spell.

The "when ... then" tension expresses a latent conflict between corporative ideal and individual aspiration. After the "then" clause is reached, nature's myriad figures disappear (Werther no longer sees them as his eyes darken), and instead of being embraced by them, Werther now embraces them in turn as the world around him rests in his soul. Werther strives to overthrow a cosmic order that subsumes him by aesthetically subsuming it under his own identity, making it into a reflection of his own soul. This desire to subordinate reality to individual experience is legitimated in the mystical tradition of projecting a God who does the same.

However, Werther's desire to mold nature aesthetically into a mirror of his own soul remains an unfulfilled longing so remote that its mere

---

[27] Hans-Peter Herrmann similarly analyzes a parallel passage in Werther's letter of August 18. Hans-Peter Herrmann, "Landschaft in Goethes 'Werther.' Zum Brief vom 18. August," in *Goethe. Vorträge aus Anlaß seines 150. Todestages*, ed. Thomas Clasen and Erwin Leibfried (Frankfurt, Bern, New York: Lang, 1984), 77-100. The tension Herrmann finds between idyllic nature (corporative ideal) and violent nature (the chaos produced by non-corporative aspirations) actually emerge much earlier in the work.

projection requires him to attribute it to another (in the "then" clause, he switches from first to second person). Moreover, the prospect of fulfilling his longing fills him with the dread of self-destruction: nature's idyllic imagery suddenly turns violent and threatens to destroy him. Transformed from independent "figures" into "appearances," nature becomes a function of Werther's own perspective; where he fails as artist, Werther succeeds in mastering nature by rendering it from (and subordinating it to) his own written viewpoint in his letters. Thus rendered, nature presents Werther in reified form with his own power and mastery (for instance, as master of the garden). The transformation of idyllic into violent nature imagery articulates the displacement of Werther's corporative ideal by his own non-corporative aspirations.

Where does this contradiction lead in the work? Why does nature's aesthetic appropriation threaten to turn violent? Before addressing these questions, I shall first try to determine more precisely what nature means for Werther. In his garden and in the valley by the brook, nature is an object of self-contemplation through aesthetic appropriation. What further aspirations (if any) does it represent, and what are their implications?

Werther's "Patriarchal Ideal"

In his letter of May 12, Werther returns to the theme of idyllic nature with his description of the spring. This passage introduces what Werther calls his "patriarchal ideal:"

> You go down a small hill and find yourself before a vault where about twenty steps descend to where the clearest water flows from marble cliffs. The little wall comprising the enclosure up above, the tall trees that cover the spot all around, the coolness of the place; all this has something seductive, something awesome.... Then the girls from the city come and fetch water, the most harmless of tasks and the most necessary, which before was performed by the daughters of kings themselves. When I sit there, the patriarchal ideal lives so vividly around me, how they, all the patriarchs, strike up acquaintance and court at the spring, and how benevolent spirits soar around the springs and fountains.[28]

---

[28] "Du gehst einen kleinen Hügel hinunter und findest dich vor einem Gewölbe, da wohl zwanzig Stufen hinabgehen, wo unten das klarste Wasser aus Marmorfelsen quillt. Die kleine Mauer, die oben umher die Einfassung

The spring's association with hill, trees, marble cliffs, the enclosure of the wall, the surrounding trees covering the spot, and its coolness suggest another nature idyll. This ancient vision of stasis in nature is intimately associated with a family archetype from the Bible in the story of Rebeccah (*Genesis* 24). Abraham, who lives in southern Canaan, sends a servant to his home town of Haran (Upper Mesopotamia) to find a wife for his son Isaac. The servant waits at the well outside town in the evening for the first woman who will let him drink from her pitcher and water his camels. Abraham's grandniece Rebeccah does so, whereupon the servant reveals his identity and mission, and eventually takes Rebeccah to Canaan to wed Isaac and become the mother of Jacob, or Israel. In *Genesis*, Israel is a family archetype organized around and ruled by patriarchs. By blending the theme of family with idyllic nature imagery, Werther uses it to project a vision of social relations that is original, natural, and harmonious.

Central to this vision is the patriarch, an authority figure. In Werther's patriarchal ideal, the traditional vision of a distant patriarchal authority brutally vindictive when disobeyed (such as the Old Testament's Yahweh Saboath) gives way to a new vision of patriarchy based on mutual love and consent. Lotte's order to her siblings to mind her sister Sophie while she is gone illustrates the new ethic: "A little sassy blond of about six said, 'Still, it's not you, Lottchen, we like you better.'"[29] The authoritarian effect is the same, but the means change from brute appeal to force to an appeal to filial love.

Werther's patriarchal ideal at the spring similarly softens corporative relations in society at large by implicitly reforming them. It suggests a time when menial tasks such as fetching water were performed by the aristocracy. This not only indicates a muted critique of the aristocracy's pursuit of harmful and needless business like the persistent hunts that ravaged farmland in Germany, it suggests a corporative social ideal: disparate strata cooperating and participating together in providing for the basic needs of all.

---

macht, die hohen Bäume, die den Platz ringsumher bedecken, die Kühle des Orts; das alles hat so was Anzügliches, was Schauerliches.... Da kommen dann die Mädchen aus der Stadt und holen Wasser, das harmloseste Geschäft und das nötigste, das ehemals die Töchter der Könige selbst verrichteten. Wenn ich da sitze, so lebt die patriarchalische Idee so lebhaft um mich, wie sie, alle die Altväter, am Brunnen Bekanntschaft machen und freien, und wie um die Brunnen und Quellen wohltätige Geister schweben." (May 12)

[29] "Eine kleine, naseweise Blondine aber, von ungefähr sechs Jahren, sagte: 'Du bists doch nicht, Lottchen, wir haben dich doch lieber.'" (June 16)

Werther contrasts this vision of corporative harmony with the social snubs he sees around him ("and then there are refugees and malevolent jokers who seem to condescend only in order to make their superiority felt all the more keenly by the poor people").[30] By contrast, Werther helps a servant girl from town at the spring to lift her jug onto her head. Despite its patrimonial condescension, this is an act of kindness. Werther's fraternization with his social inferiors represents a new, modern strategy in the history of domination and exploitation, a sort of "absolutism with a human face."

In his study of patriarchal history, Bengt A. Sørensen shows that love came to supplant fear as a means of social control in the eighteenth century.[31] Just as the ideal family father gradually changed from a strict, distant pedant into a warm, caring parent, so the Enlightened despot as patriarchal sovereign (*Landesvater*) came to be expected to win legitimacy through the love of his subjects. Patriarchal authority bestowed by nature was never questioned, but its ideal means of articulation and legitimation switched from authoritarian edict to something verging on personal consent.

The new ethic was hardly revolutionary. Authoritarian relations and exploitation not only remain unquestioned in *Genesis* (where slaves serve the family of Israel), they appear original there and therefore natural. Werther's good deed in helping the servant with her jug in no way alters his privileged status. In fact, in placing the jug on her head, Werther symbolically loads her with housework, reiterating traditional patterns of gender- and class-specific domination. By calling her a "young servant girl" (*junges Dienstmädchen*), socially disenfranchised at any age due to her servile and sexual status, Werther reiterates her subordination as a woman and as a servant. Werther's supercilious references to "people of this sort" as well as the servant's own protestations against accepting help from him only serve to show, in Werther's words, "how necessary the difference among the estates is."

Nature at the spring is closely associated with an image of family as a metaphor for a better society. Werther's patriarchal ideal implies paternal (or state) authority based on love and consent rather than fear. This reflects a new eighteenth-century ethic of absolutism reformed to show a friendly face. Prevailing patterns of domination under a re-

---

[30] "Und dann gibts Flüchtlinge und üble Spaßvögel, die sich herabzulassen scheinen, um ihren Übermut dem armen Volke desto empfindlicher zu machen." (May 15)

[31] Bengt A. Sørensen, *Herrschaft und Zärtlichkeit* (Munich: Beck, 1984), 11-61.

formed absolutism appear as original as the story of Rebeccah and as natural and eternal as the *locus amoenus* at the spring. This is the ideological kernel of Werther's patriarchal ideal.

Werther's blending of family ideals with idyllic nature imagery continues in his letter of May 26 about his "chosen home" Wahlheim, a village far from the city where Werther finds the space to formulate his own sense of identity. Elements of idyllic nature reappear at Wahlheim, which is enclosed by cooling linden trees. Werther cooks his peas there, incorporating what he calls features of patriarchy into his lifestyle.

Werther spots two children sitting on the ground, one on the other's lap. He seats himself on a nearby plow and sketches the fraternal scene along with "the next fence, the shed door and a few broken wagon wheels..., everything the way it stood." The success of his drawing "strengthened me in my resolve to stick only to nature" and to disregard conventions, since they destroy "the true feeling of nature and the true expression thereof."[32]

Of course, nothing about what Werther sketches is natural. The children are motionless because they have been ordered to sit still by their mother; fence and shed door are means of enclosing nature spaces and controlling environments; and the wagon wheels as well as the plow Werther sits on are traditional tools for exploiting nature. All frame Wahlheim itself, the enclosed spot (with its natural aura) that Werther associates with the family intimacy he attributes to the children he draws.

What Werther means by sticking to nature is not sketching nature itself, but rather drawing in a naturalistic way everything as it appears "without adding to it the slightest of myself."[33] This fiction is transparent. Faced with wild nature imagery on May 10 in the valley by the brook, Werther is aesthetically paralyzed by it. Only in an environment as thoroughly tamed as Wahlheim is Werther able to overcome nature's hidden terror. From the solitary perspective of his plow, Werther sketches broken wheels and other images of stasis that inform Wahlheim. Sticking to nature means banishing conflict and change by transforming nature into a vision of timeless family intimacy from the perspective of the isolated individual. "All the tumult is relieved," Werther writes of the mother of the boys he sketches, "by the sight of such a creature, who

---

[32] "... den nächsten Zaun, ein Scheunentor und einige gebrochene Wagenräder..., alles, wie es hinter einander stand.... [Das] bestärkte mich in meinem Vorsatze, mich künftig allein an die Natur zu halten." Conventions destroy "das wahre Gefühl von Natur und den wahren Ausdruck derselben." (May 26)

[33] "...ohne das mindeste von dem Meinen hinzuzutun." (May 26)

follows in happy tranquility the narrow circle of her existence, manages from one day to the next, sees the leaves fall and thinks only that the winter is coming."[34] At Wahlheim, Werther escapes the tumultuous conflicts and confrontations of life in town by imagining the peasant mother as a simple creature enjoying an animal-like existence within her family circle at one with the cycles of nature. Wahlheim represents family life as a natural cycle that obviates conflict and change.

This simple, natural lifestyle is associated with a traditional way of life. The peasants are all in the field producing the surplus that makes it possible for Werther to sketch their town in solitude. An innkeeper provides him with table, chair, and coffee. Werther takes advantage of the leisure time and creature comforts thus afforded him to indulge in traditional pursuits of the privileged (reading and sketching). Wahlheim suggests a well-ordered corporative hierarchy without any hint of conflict.

In view of his experiences at Wahlheim, Werther issues an almost programmatic call for a new natural sense of identity transcending the conventions that would bind it. If conventions undermine nature, then the individual who wishes to establish his or her own identity must shun conventional pursuits and seek instead a sense of purpose on the fringes of corporative society. This is not only tantamount to a declaration of independence on the part of the bourgeois individual from corporative society, it is also a plaintive statement of crisis. "Oh my friends!" Werther says,

> why does the stream of genius so seldom break out, so seldom roar in with high floods and shake your marvelling soul? — Dear friends, there the impassive gentlemen live on both sides of the shore, whose garden houses, tulip beds, and cabbage fields would be destroyed, who therefore know how to ward off in time the menacing future danger with dams and drainage ditches.[35]

---

[34] "[S]o lindert all den Tumult der Anblick eines solchen Geschöpfs, das in glücklicher Gelassenheit den engen Kreis seines Daseins hingeht, von einem Tage zum andern sich durchhilft, die Blätter abfallen sieht und nichts dabei denkt, als daß der Winter kommt." (May 27)

[35] "O meine Freunde! warum der Strom des Genies so selten ausbricht, so selten in hohen Fluten hereinbraust und eure staunende Seele erschüttert? — Liebe Freunde, da wohnen die gelassenen Herren auf beiden Seiten des Ufers, denen ihre Gartenhäuschen, Tulpenbeete und Krautfelder zugrunde gehen würden, die daher inzeiten mit Dämmen und Ableiten der künftig drohenden Gefahr abzuwehren wissen." (May 26)

Werther uses a nature metaphor (the stream of genius) to illustrate his thesis that natural creativity is stymied by the artificial dams of social convention. But Werther himself is one of the "impassive gentlemen on both sides of the shore." Both in sketching and describing the scene at Wahlheim, he molds nature space into a static scene sheltered and preserved by walls, fences, and trees. The garden houses, tulip beds, and cabbage fields Werther mentions smack of his own alcove in his garden and the inn garden in Wahlheim where he picks his peas. Both Werther's garden and Wahlheim are located on heights overlooking the valley below, and both are potentially threatened by rising water levels. The stream of genius that roars in high floods threatens to inundate Werther's own idyllic nature spots and destroy the patriarchal ideal associated with them. Werther's separate sense of identity on the margins of traditional society becomes a menacing future danger threatening Werther himself.

For Werther, Wahlheim is informed by images of idyllic nature and family, components of his patriarchal ideal. It offers him a chance to express himself artistically in a way transcending social convention. This very transcendence poses a problem, however. Instead of projecting a positive social alternative, Werther's aesthetic vision of Wahlheim affirms a traditional social ideal that excludes any prospect of change. With no alternative but the empty form of alterity itself, Werther faces a frightening void on society's fringes. The violent nature of individual expression — projecting the power latent in Werther's own artistic endeavors — threatens not only social conventions, but Werther's own vision of family intimacy in idyllic nature: in his later letters, the family he meets at Wahlheim becomes desperate as nature turns bleak and wintry. Werther's articulation of an alternative identity at Wahlheim is a sterile mirage behind which looms the specter of a violent chaos that threatens Werther himself.

The Appropriation of Women: Lotte

Goethe's *Werther* is less a love story than an exploration of individual identity. Several key themes are introduced in the ten letters that precede Werther's first meeting with Lotte (Werther's isolation in nature, his social alienation, the family/nature ideal implicit in his patriarchal ideal, his fear of chaotic nature). The relationship between Lotte and Werther develops these themes.

Werther first mentions Lotte in passing in his letter of May 17. "It's said," he says of her father, "that it's a joy for the soul to see him among his children, of which he has nine; especially much is made of his oldest daughter."[36] Appearing parenthetically in a reference to her father, Lotte becomes the discursive object of anonymous opinion within Werther's social circle. This anonymity serves to cancel any hint of Lotte's individuality. Instead, she represents a value apparently shared among Werther's peers: the joyous vision of children surrounding a patriarch. Before Werther ever meets her, Lotte already begins to symbolize home and family for him.

Lotte's initial appeal for Werther is not personal. He literally fails to describe her ("and still I am unable to tell you how she is perfect"), using conventional formulations such as "an angel" before dismissing them as "vile nonsense," "tiresome abstractions that do not express one feature of her self."[37] But when it comes to depicting Lotte surrounded by her siblings, he readily finds the words:

> I went through the courtyard to the well-constructed house, and when I had climbed the steps outside and entered the door, I beheld the most charming scene I ever saw. In the antechamber six children, from eleven to two years of age, were crowding around a girl of attractive shape, average height, who had on a simple white dress with pink bows on arm and breast. She held a loaf of black bread and cut off for each of her little ones all around a piece in proportion to age and appetite, gave it to each with such affection, and each called out so unaffectedly his "Thank you!"[38]

---

[36] "Man sagt, es soll eine Seelenfreude sein, ihn unter seinen Kindern zu sehen, deren er neun hat; besonders macht man viel Wesens von seiner ältesten Tochter." (May 17)

[37] "Einen Engel! — Pfui! ... Und doch bin ich nicht imstande, dir zu sagen, wie sie vollkommen ist.... Das ist alles garstiges Gewäsch, was ich da von ihr sage, leidige Abstraktionen, die nicht einen Zug ihres Selbst ausdrücken." (June 16)

[38] "Ich ging durch den Hof nach dem wohlgebauten Hause, und da ich die vorliegenden Treppen hinaufgestiegen war und in die Tür trat, fiel mir das reizendste Schauspiel in die Augen, das ich je gesehen habe. In dem Vorsaale wimmelten sechs Kinder, von eilf zu zwei Jahren, um ein Mädchen von schöner Gestalt, mittlerer Größe, die ein simples weißes Kleid, mit blaßroten Schleifen an Arm und Brust, anhatte. Sie hielt ein schwarzes Brot und schnitt ihren Kleinen rings herum jedem sein Stück nach Proportion ihres Alters und Appetits ab, gab's jedem mit solcher Freundlichkeit, und jedes rief so ungekünstelt sein: 'Danke!'" (June 16)

This first impression of Lotte is lasting for both reader and Werther alike. It is a widely illustrated scene from the novel, and Werther later procures Lotte's pink bow as a memento, suggesting the importance of this moment in defining her significance for him. Its salient feature is Lotte's context of home and family. Before mentioning Lotte, Werther describes the physical setting of her home in considerable detail. This setting frames the central scene of Lotte mothering her siblings. What apparently draws Werther to Lotte is not her personality or sexuality, but her role as surrogate mother on the stage of home and family. "What ecstasy for my soul it is," he intones, "to see her in the circle of the sweet vivacious children, her eight brothers and sisters!"[39]

The structure of this statement, which sums up Lotte's attraction for Werther, is revealing. The second clause in this sentence ("to see her") depends on the first ("What ecstasy for my soul it is"). In terms of both sequential and structural priority, the emphasis falls on the first clause, which mentions Lotte only by implication, focusing instead on Werther himself. Lotte is reduced to a perceptual object meaningful primarily in the context of her siblings. She is subsumed under Werther's concern with his own feelings of pleasure. On the stage of her family performance, she becomes an object of Werther's aesthetic entertainment and enjoyment by virtue of what she represents for him: the values of hearth and home, of the intimate family circle in the private sphere.

Lotte's remarks about literature on the way to the ball confirm her representation of egoism as well as home and family. "And I like the author best," she says, "in whom I rediscover my world, in whom things go on as they do around me, and whose story is still as interesting and heartfelt as my own domestic life, which may not be a paradise, but is still on the whole a source of unspeakable happiness."[40] While the editor ironically distances himself from such sentiments in a footnote, Werther is deeply moved by them. Lotte does not read in order to discover new horizons, but to experience the familiarity of her own world. Her preoccupation with herself blends with her orientation toward home and family, reminiscent of the Wahlheim peasant mother's contentment with the narrow circle of her family existence. For Werther,

---

[39] "Welch eine Wonne das für meine Seele ist, sie in dem Kreise der lieben muntern Kinder, ihrer acht Geschwister zu sehen!" (June 16)

[40] "Und der Autor ist mir der liebste, in dem ich meine Welt wiederfinde, bei dem es zugeht wie um mich, und dessen Geschichte mir doch so interessant und herzlich wird als mein eigen häuslich Leben, das freilich kein Paradies, aber doch im ganzen eine Quelle unsäglicher Glückseligkeit ist." (June 16)

both women represent an ideal of motherhood in the self-contained private sphere of home and family.

This private sphere is intimately associated with wild nature far from the city. Lotte lives in a sylvan setting, a hunting lodge owned by the prince, where Lotte's father received permission to move after the death of his wife, since city and the magistrate's house (*Amthaus*) there reminded him too much of her. Before dying, her mother prevailed on Lotte to assume "the heart of a mother and the eye of a mother ... and for your father the faithfulness and obedience of a wife" and to be happy together with Albert.[41] This symbolic reconstruction of the intimate family circle, with Lotte as surrogate mother, takes place far from city and magisterial seat, which are associated with the pain of family dissolution. By implication, the notion of family conflicts with the idea of corporative authority in the public sphere, requiring a historic relocation far from the city. At the same time, the family is divorced from the arena of production and social interaction, becoming the locus of consumption, nurture, and reproduction.

Werther calls the magistrate's domicile in the woods his "hermitage" or "little kingdom." As a hermitage, Lotte's home appeals to Werther's preference for solitude in nature. As a kingdom, it suggests the linguistic entwinement of family and corporative dominion in the eighteenth century. The family as kingdom implicitly claims autonomy for the private household (or private individual within it) from public authority, but it also projects an authoritarian hierarchy onto the private sphere, represented by the magistrate's continuing role as public servant and the prince's ownership of his new home. The ideal corporative dominion as family (with benevolent patriarchal sovereign) expresses this contradiction, implicitly lifting private sphere autonomy by projecting princely authority onto all aspects of life. In describing the family circle as hermitage and kingdom, Werther idealizes private sphere isolation in nature, where an independent sense of identity can develop, while yearning for a corporative harmony governed by a benevolent central authority that obviates the private/public split.

Werther's projection of Lotte in terms of her father's home in nature unites both ideals. Since the magistrate is conspicuously absent, Lotte's wifely role of authority within the household is amplified. Authority is birthright: as the eldest, Lotte inherits authority from her deceased mother. In her absence, Lotte in turn bestows responsibility for the household and authority over the children upon the eldest sister after

---

[41] "...das Herz einer Mutter und das Aug einer Mutter ... und für deinen Vater die Treue und den Gehorsam einer Frau." (September 10)

her. The traditional notion of authority as birthright is tempered in Lotte's case by her merit: since she combines so much goodness with firmness, she deserves her position. The corporative ideal that personal merit goes hand in glove with authority by birthright is realized in the person of Lotte.

To his delight, Lotte tentatively integrates Werther into her family when she tells her brother to shake his "cousin's" hand. When Werther questions the sobriquet "cousin," Lotte insists that her family has many relations and that he could be one of them. At Wahlheim, Werther is excluded by social distance from the peasant family he meets. He buys the privilege of observing it from the fringes with friendliness and bribes (the coins he gives the children). But with Lotte, there is no social obstacle to entering the family circle.

The key is acquiring Lotte herself, and Werther begins to do so from the moment he meets her. He writes of her as a "treasure hidden in the quiet region."[42] Nature's unexplored reaches contain resources ripe for the taking. Lotte becomes an object of value claimable as property.

In particular, Werther appropriates her aesthetically. While watching the spectacle of Lotte distributing bread to siblings, he declares that "my whole soul rested on the figure, the tone, the deportment,"[43] analyzing her into component forms subsumed under the introspective observer. Similarly, on the way to the ball, after dismissing the presence of the others in the coach, he reduces Lotte to a set of impressions:

> How I grazed in the black eyes during the conversation — how the lively lips and the fresh, vibrant cheeks drew my whole soul — how, engrossed in the magnificent meaning of her speech, I often missed the words with which she expressed herself.... In short, I got out of the carriage like someone dreaming when we stopped before the summer house, and was so lost in dreams out in the darkening world that I hardly paid attention to the music that resonated down to us from the brightly lit hall.[44]

---

[42] "Ich ... wäre vielleicht nie hingekommen, hätte mir der Zufall nicht den Schatz entdeckt, der in der stillen Gegend verborgen liegt." (June 16)

[43] "[M]eine ganze Seele ruhte auf der Gestalt, dem Tone, dem Betragen." (June 16)

[44] "Wie ich mich unter dem Gespräche in den schwarzen Augen weidete - wie die lebendigen Lippen und die frischen, muntern Wangen meine ganze Seele anzogen - wie ich, in den herrlichen Sinn ihrer Rede ganz versunken, oft gar die Worte nicht hörte, mit denen sie sich ausdrückte... Kurz, ich stieg aus dem Wagen wie ein Träumender, als wir vor dem Lusthause stille hielten, und war

Lotte is reduced to eyes, lips, and cheeks, while her words are blocked out in favor of the marvelous meaning of her paeans to home and family. For Werther, Lotte becomes an object of aesthetic reflection, a disembodied set of values and images that enhances his own proclivity toward losing himself in reveries. As she vanishes from his discourse, his egoistic focus becomes clear. By concentrating on his impressions of Lotte, Werther loses touch with those around him, including Lotte herself.

This poses an interesting problem at the heart of Werther's competitive relationship with Albert. Werther appropriates Lotte and all she means for him not as a potential wife, for this would imply the philistine duties and responsibilities he berates in Albert, her fiance. He appropriates her aesthetically, as his property in terms of the set of images and ideals that she represents for him. As a coveted natural treasure, Lotte ultimately derives from and reinforces his own sense of isolation in nature. Predicated on an aesthetic solution to the social conflicts and barriers he observes, Werther's desire for Lotte precludes an active challenge to Albert's claim to her. Such a challenge would deflate her value for Werther, since it would open the door to the world of competing and conflicting interests from which her family context seems to offer respite. This helps to explain why Werther fails to capitalize upon his ultimate realization that Lotte loves him.

At the same time, Werther shares Albert's bourgeois acquisitiveness, his drive to possess "precisely me, the property of another" (as Lotte puts it). Whereas aesthetic appropriation in medieval *minnesang* or early modern poetry presented no challenge to actuality, in the eighteenth century materiality enters aesthetic discourse. Werther's aesthetic appropriation of Lotte implies his desire to actually possess her. This leads him into an insoluble quandary: he must have Lotte in order to realize his dreams, yet possessing her would destroy them. The aesthetic ideals that Lotte signifies for him are undermined by the very ethic of possessive and manipulative egoism from which they derive.

After arriving at the ball, Werther dances with Lotte. The two most prominent social dances at the time were the *contredanse* and the minuet. The former derived from English country dances, while the latter was taken from French folk dance and refined into elegance at the court of Louis XIV. Both were open-couple dances involving partners who held hands. The *contredanse* involved a complex choreography.

---

so in Träumen rings in der dämmernden Welt verloren, daß ich auf die Musik kaum achtete, die uns von dem erleuchteten Saal herunter entgegenschallte." (June 16)

Partners frequently changed hands in patterns that included the entire group on the dance floor. The group performed as one, reenacting the corporative ideal of all of society's disparate sectors acting together in harmony. While partners did not change hands in the minuet, the couples all moved as one, performing the same ceremonious steps simultaneously. Like the *contredanse*, the minuet reenacted the corporative ideal of universal harmony. While balls were fun, they also served an important social function: they reaffirmed in dance the conventions that held society together.

Werther defies this corporative context by striving to appropriate Lotte for himself wherever possible. He becomes her partner in the waltz, a form of dance newly derived from German folk dancing. Spurned in aristocratic circles, these dances were still unfamiliar enough to the new bourgeoisie to be danced clumsily. The waltz broke with the courtly tradition of open-couple dancing; the partners held each other in modern closed-couple style. Moreover, individual couples performed their movements independently, obviating the necessity of group participation and cohesion.[45] More appropriate to an individualistic form of social organization, they subverted the group cohesion of traditional dances while enacting the symbolic appropriation of one's partner.

Notably, Werther waltzes unusually well. He waits with Lotte until the clumsier couples leave, finally remaining the only ones on the floor aside from another couple. "I was no longer human," Werther crows. "To have the sweetest creature in my arms and to fly around with her like storm weather, so that everything all around vanished."[46] Waltzing virtually alone with Lotte transforms Werther from a person presumably into something divine. While the people who dance the minuet and other traditional dances together reiterate corporative society, Werther's divine waltzing articulates an alternative individuality and identity. While waltzing with Lotte like a storm, the corporative context of the ball vanishes; all that remains is Werther firmly in possession of the creature in his arms. His acquisitive actions carry unmistakably destructive overtones.

After waltzing, Werther feeds Lotte hoarded orange slices, but begrudges the pieces she gives to "an immodest neighbor." Werther considers the orange slices theirs. The others at the ball, whom Werther

---

[45] Mary Clarke and Clement Crisp, *The History of Dance* (New York: Crown Publishers, 1981), 96-101.

[46] "Ich war kein Mensch mehr. Das liebenswürdigste Geschöpf in den Armen zu haben und mit ihr herumzufliegen wie Wetter, daß alles rings umher verging." (June 16)

had banished while talking in the carriage and while waltzing, are at best distant neighbors with no right to interrupt Werther and Lotte or to claim whatever they have. In using images of household and property, Werther builds an aura of privacy around himself and Lotte while placing an implicit claim on her. As his sole waltzing partner, she becomes "a girl to which I laid claim," and he vows never to let such a person waltz with anyone else. As prospective property, Lotte is reduced to the relative anonymity of "girl" or "creature."

The ball is suddenly interrupted by a violent thunderstorm. The music stops, and some of the women weep, huddle, or hide their heads. The novel is based on events in the Lahn Valley near Wetzlar, not far from the Wetterau near Frankfurt with its spectacular weather patterns. Since thunderstorms are not uncommon in the region to which the novel alludes, and since the small-town women there might be presumed to be quite familiar with nature's moods in the surrounding countryside, their terrified reactions appear implausible. Clearly, there is more to the storm and the terror it evokes than meets the eye.

The context offers a clue. Just before the storm, Werther's advances grow so blatant that one woman shakes her finger warningly at Lotte and mentions Albert's name. Lotte explains that she is practically engaged to Albert, something Werther already knew. Nevertheless, it still shocks him, "because I had not yet thought of it in relation to her who in so few moments had grown so valuable to me."[47] This suggests that there are two Lottes: next to the one of value to Werther as incarnation of home and family in nature is another one whose quaint lifestyle and conventional aspirations include marrying Albert because he is a good person. The problem for Werther is reconciling this prosaic Lotte with the aestheticized one. She represents value for Werther, and something of value (whether aesthetic or otherwise) for the new bourgeoisie is an object of possession. Albert's status as Lotte's fiance represents a rival claim to her possession.

This prospective conflict of interests disrupts the dance. Confused, Werther blunders into the wrong couple, producing chaos. In articulating a private-sphere framework for possessing Lotte, Werther formulates an alternative to the corporative ideal of social harmony without actually destroying it; but in taking the next step and confronting the prospect of a competitive property struggle with a rival, Werther demolishes its social basis. The struggle of atomized individuals among themselves is suited to incipient capitalism, but anathema to a society that depends for

---

[47] "...weil ich es noch nicht im Verhältnis auf sie, die mir in so wenig Augenblicken so wert geworden war, gedacht hatte." (June 16)

its stability on subordinating individual aspirations to traditional duties and prerogatives. When Werther realizes the conflict he faces, he acts out its social implications by disrupting the traditional dance.

This conflict assumes cosmic proportions with the onset of the storm. Werther first notices it on the horizon just before meeting Lotte, and suspects that it will disrupt the ball. The danger grows as Werther tries to appropriate Lotte. The storm frames Werther's aesthetic appropriation of Lotte, the reiteration of his own alienation in doing so, the realization that he must compete to possess her, and the chaos that follows the disruption of the dance.

As such, it seems more than a poetic figure paralleling the story line and mirroring Werther's own inner state of mind. In an age still attuned to the traditional premise that nature reflects God's will, the storm's disruption of the dance likely signals divine disapprobation of events. This frightening prospect explains the terror on the part of the dancers. "When a misfortune or something frightening surprises us in the midst of pleasure," Werther surmises, it has a stronger impact than usual.[48] This "misfortune or something frightening" signifies more than mere weather. The pleasure it disrupts is the ball, a formal reiteration of social convention, and what it causes is social chaos. "Three ladies fled the row, followed by their gentlemen," Werther observes, "the disorder became general, and the music stopped."[49] The fear and chaos produced by the storm reflect a negative attitude toward processes that threaten the conventional social order, processes that Werther develops in trying to appropriate Lotte.

Most of the revelers escape to a room with shutters and curtains designed to block out the storm. In this private retreat, Lotte reconstitutes the group in the image of her own home with her counting game. After seating people in a circle around her, she goes around the circle pointing to each, and each names a consecutive number starting with one. Any hesitation or error is punished with a slap.

Lotte's game approximates her parental role in the circle of her siblings. As authority figure surrounded by contextual inferiors in need of discipline, she appropriately punishes each, just as she proportionately distributes bread to her siblings. The special severity of her slaps to Werther distinguishes him from his peers as particularly meriting her attention in her role as surrogate parent, since it was Werther whose

---

[48] "Wenn uns ein Unglück oder etwas Schreckliches im Vergnügen überrascht..." (June 16)

[49] "Drei Frauenzimmer liefen aus der Reihe, denen ihre Herren folgten, die Unordnung wurde allgemein, und die Musik hörte auf." (June 16)

efforts to appropriate her disrupted the dance. The success of Lotte's game suggests a vision of the intimate family circle supplanting the dissolution of the traditional order in the storm of events. "Over the slaps," Lotte declares, "they've forgotten weather and everything!"[50]

By symbolically reconstructing the intimate family circle, Lotte staves off the threat of the storm outside. The storm's dissipation is cosmic tribute to her resolution of a menacing situation:

> It thundered off to the side, and the magnificent rain pattered on the land, and the most refreshing aroma rose up to us in all the fullness of a warm draft. She stood leaning on her elbows, her gaze penetrated the area; she looked heavenward and at me, I saw her tearful eye, she placed her hand on mine and said, "Klopstock!"[51]

The reference here to Klopstock's "Frühlingsfeier" suggests the great chain of being, a vision of nature reaffirming the cosmic hierarchy of worm, man, and God. The language of family, nature, and corporative dominion are reconciled here for the last time in the novel.

Werther's Suicide

Werther spends a few happy weeks in Lotte's company before Albert's arrival. "Never before was I happier," he notes on July 24, "never before was my feeling for nature, down to the pebble, to the smallest grass, fuller and more intense."[52] Lotte's proximity enhances Werther's sense of nature, which in turn leads him back to her. On June 21, Werther compares nature's nebulous distances with prospects for the future. The search for fulfillment of the solitary self in nature leads to frustration: once distant horizons are reached, their promise fades, while inner poverty and limitations remain.

---

[50] "Über die Ohrfeigen haben sie Wetter und alles vergessen!" (June 16)

[51] "Es donnerte abseitwärts, und der herrliche Regen säuselte auf das Land, und der erquickendste Wohlgeruch stieg in aller Fülle einer warmen Luft zu uns auf. Sie stand auf ihren Ellenbogen gestützt, ihr Blick durchdrang die Gegend; sie sah gen Himmel und auf mich, ich sah ihr Auge tränenvoll, sie legte ihre Hand auf die meinige und sagte: 'Klopstock!' (June 16)

[52] "Noch nie war ich glücklicher, noch nie war meine Empfindung an der Natur, bis aufs Steinchen, aufs Gräschen herunter, voller und inniger...." (July 24)

The answer is to return to home and family. "So the most restless vagabond finally longs again for his fatherland," Werther notes, "and finds in his cabin, at the breast of his spouse, in the circle of his children, in tasks designed to preserve them the ecstasy that he sought in vain in the wide world."[53] Intimately associated with this ideal of hearth and home, Wahlheim is on the way to Lotte, "and once I am there, it's only another half hour to her! ... In a flash I am there."[54] Werther's wanderings in nature focus on the family ideal he associates with Lotte's home. "How often in my wide wanderings have I seen the hunting lodge that now contains all my wishes, now from the mountain, now from the plain across the river!"[55] After leading Werther on his walks over mountains, across plains, through forests, and back up the hill to Wahlheim, nature itself points the way back to home and family — if he can possess Lotte.

Herein lies a hidden danger. Werther compares Lotte to the magnetic mountain of which his grandmother had told him: ships that come too near lose their nails and fall apart, drowning all aboard. While Lotte represents the promise of a treasure hidden in nature, its irresistible magnetism could turn into a frightening, destructive force.

The magnetic-mountain image illustrates Werther's growing realization that there is no way out. Although Werther is irresistibly drawn to Lotte, Albert has a prior claim to her. Struggling with Albert over Lotte would destroy what she means to him: a return to home and family, to an imagined domicile in the past. After leaving court, Werther revisits his home town, where to his deep disappointment everything has changed. Lotte appeals to him because she signifies a time before change, an idealized intimate family circle at one with the original cycles of nature. Possessing her would unleash the forces of change he detests: the struggle between competing interests over property, a central force of modern change displacing the old corporative order. Werther refuses to participate in this process by competing with Albert for Lotte.

---

[53] "So sehnt sich der unruhigste Vagabund zuletzt wieder nach seinem Vaterlande und findet in seiner Hütte, an der Brust seiner Gattin, in dem Kreise seiner Kinder, in den Geschäften zu ihrer Erhaltung die Wonne, die er in der weiten Welt vergebens suchte." (June 21)

[54] "...und wenn ich nun da bin, ists nur noch eine halbe Stunde zu ihr! ... Zuck! so bin ich dort." (July 26)

[55] "Wie oft habe ich das Jagdhaus, das nun alle meine Wünsche einschließt, auf meinen weiten Wanderungen, bald vom Berge, bald von der Ebne über den Fluß gesehen!" (June 21)

This in turn conflicts with Werther's egoistic and acquisitive nature on the fringes of traditional society. Werther must possess Lotte or perish. His nature responds to the repression of his desire for Lotte with violence. Someone who commits suicide out of despair, Werther argues in his letter of August 12, dies of natural causes as surely as someone who succumbs to fever. "Nature finds no escape from the labyrinth of muddled and conflicting forces," he concludes, "and the person must die."[56]

Werther's argument that nature is responsible for violent acts such as the suicide of a young girl or the revolt of an oppressed people suggests a latent fear of the social processes behind such events. Instead of understanding violent behavior as a response to changing conditions, it is equated with nature itself, obfuscating its origins. Werther's search for a home in Lotte's company has an egoistic premise: Lotte and the family she represents appear as private property that first must be won in competitive struggle with Albert. Even though Werther does not accept the challenge, he is irrevocably caught in the logic of the competitive situation and finally turns its violence against himself, in accordance with nature. Represented as nature, the struggle of all against all for possession of private property appears primordial and inevitable. It also appears terrible in its destructivity, suggesting a profound fear of the processes of modern change it represents.

Werther's letter of August 18 contains the turning point in his relationship to nature and in the novel overall. "The inner glowing, holy life of nature," Werther writes, has become "an eternally devouring, eternally ruminating monster."[57] In structure and content, Werther's letter of August 18 parallels his letter of May 10. In both letters, the "when ... then" clauses that articulate Werther's vision of a great chain of being give way to violent nature imagery that threatens Werther himself. Each letter refers in the language of nature to a corporative ideal of harmonious hierarchy undermined by an experienced reality of conflict among competing egoistic interests.

In his letter of August 18, Werther identifies these forces with change. "There is no moment," he intones, "that does not devour you and your loved ones around you, no moment in which you are not perforce a destroyer; the most harmless stroll costs a thousand poor

---

[56] "Die Natur findet keinen Ausweg aus dem Labyrinthe der verworrenen und widersprechenden Kräfte, und der Mensch muß sterben." (August 12)

[57] "Das innere glühende, heilige Leben der Natur ... ein ewig verschlingendes, ewig wiederkäuendes Ungeheuer." (August 18)

worms their lives."[58] By contrast, Werther's ideal of home and family is based on preserving unchanged the homeland, cabin, spouse, and circle of children to which the vagabond finally returns. Lotte appeals to Werther most when dancing "as if she thought about nothing else, felt nothing else; and at this moment everything else surely fades away before her."[59] Preserving the moment (and thereby thwarting change) is important to Werther's project of self-preoccupation. His realization that the world is constantly changing by virtue of devolutionary processes in nature brings him to the point of despair. He identifies with these changes, calling himself a destroyer of nature: on August 18, he realizes that his own desire to aesthetically subsume the world under his ego, still projected on May 10 as the power of nature itself, leads to chaos and destruction. His own natural non-corporative aspirations destroy his natural corporative ideal. Because he never envisions a positive alternative to the corporative order, Werther becomes the victim rather than the agent of social change.

Werther's vision of universal destruction in nature in his letter of December 12 just before committing suicide culminates the novel's violent nature imagery. During a storm, Werther ventures onto a cliff, from which he sees that the river has completely flooded his valley, turning it into a wind-swept sea. This is the same valley in which Werther had envisioned his cosmic hierarchies in his letters of May 10 and August 18. A place where he had rested under a willow with Lotte is flooded together with the area around her home. Even Wahlheim and his garden alcove seem threatened.

This closing image of nature turned violent indicates despair in the face of a swirling tide of changing events. Lotte's home, Wahlheim, the garden, and the valley, all locations of harmonious integrity in family and society, are threatened or destroyed. Werther's reference in his letter of May 26 to the stream of genius flooding garden houses, tulip beds, and cabbage fields is realized here. An ominous signal of violent nature before Werther ever meets Lotte is carried to fruition. Isolated on the cliff, Werther surveys the scene of his earlier hopes and desires, now transformed into a frightening swirl of destruction. Werther's search for an alternative identity in nature ultimately culminates in violence and chaos.

---

[58] "Da ist kein Augenblick, der dich nicht verzehre und die Deinigen um dich her, kein Augenblick, da du nicht ein Zerstörer bist, sein mußt; der harmloseste Spaziergang kostet tausend armen Würmchen das Leben." (August 18)

[59] "...als wenn sie sonst nichts dächte, nichts empfände; und in dem Augenblicke gewiß schwindet alles andere vor ihr." (June 16)

Werther is a complex and contradictory work from which it is difficult to draw facile conclusions. This is partly due to the difficulty of the work's subject matter: the problem of reconciling a corporative ideal of social harmony with modern conflict among competing individuals and their concomitant isolation on the periphery of traditional society. The novel discusses this problem without offering a solution, and this is perhaps what made it so disturbing in its day.

Central to the novel is a discussion of Werther's search for identity and what it might lead to. From his first pronouncement on how happy he is to be gone, Werther searches for alternative identities, primarily in nature. The key nature images in the novel are Werther's garden, his valley, the spring, Wahlheim, and Lotte's hunting-lodge home (including Lotte herself). All are associated with wild or idyllic nature imagery far from the despised city, and all are located close together. Werther carves out complementary identities in each.

In nature, Werther articulates the patriarchal ideal behind his reform project. By blending the language of family and corporative dominion with images of corporative harmony and natural stasis, Werther projects an ethic of patriarchal authority based on kindness and love rather than compulsion and fear. Lotte incorporates Werther's family ideal. In a kingdom isolated in the woods, her father's family — over which Lotte wields a surrogate authority that is absolute — represents a social microcosm of what could be: harmony based on meeting the needs of each member in exchange for absolute obedience to an authority grounded in benevolence yet firmness.

Lotte's own aspirations are limited to hearth and home. As child-rearer and prospective child-bearer, she teaches children to obey a central authority legitimated as benevolent, just as she is a dutiful wife to her father and later to Albert. There is nothing new in this vision. Since the sixteenth century, Protestant writers such as Martin Luther and Paul Rebhuhn had attempted to limit women to reproductive roles within the family, simultaneously divorcing the family from its role in production.[60] The ideological function of such writings was to liberate the sphere of production from a traditional division of labor defined by

---

[60] Sigrid Brauner argues convincingly that the writings of Luther, Rebhuhn, and Hans Sachs on witches were designed to redefine female gender in a way that removed women from social participation, confining them to roles within home and family. See Sigrid Brauner, "Frightened Shrews and Fearless Wives: The Concept of the Witch in Early Modern German Texts 1487-1560" (Diss. UC-Berkeley, 1989). The idealization of women as homebodies in the eighteenth century amounts to a parallel discourse on female gender, the reverse side of the same coin.

corporative custom and law, opening it to penetration by market forces. The (fictive) rise of the intimate family circle in the private sphere and the (equally fictive) elimination of women from the workplace in writings since the late Middle Ages coincided with a new-bourgeois interest in the decline of corporative control over production.

Werther's obsession with Lotte projects a vision in which the nuclear family would displace the estates as the cornerstone of society. Projected onto the state as a model of order and harmony, Lotte's idealized home life would obviate the latent conflicts and contradictions that Werther deplores among the estates. Still, the fundamental ethic of absolutism — obedience to state authority — would remain unquestioned and even enjoy a new legitimacy based on respect for benevolent territorial sovereigns who protect and provide for their subjects.

This vision buttresses a traditional corporative order threatened by inherent tensions. Werther's patriarchal ideal is designed not to undermine the authority of the princes he reveres (like Count von C.), but to restore it through reforms. However, Werther cannot realize his reform project without possessing Lotte, which presents him with an insoluble quandary: he cannot eliminate his rival Albert without destroying Lotte's value to him — the hope of using the family model to reconcile conflict and restore cosmic harmony. Werther calls the logic of this situation his "sickness unto death whereby nature is so afflicted" that it cannot recover; it is not a moral choice, but a necessity arising from nature itself.[61] The inner, natural origins of Werther's acquisitive aspirations and the frustration of realizing them emerge in the contemporary theme of the torn heart. Seeing Albert "in the possession of so many perfections ... would have torn apart my heart,"[62] Werther declares. *Werther* is one of the first German novels to articulate this modern theme.

Confronted in his letters of May 10 and August 18 with the contradiction between a traditional ideology of social harmony and a contemporary practice of confrontation among atomized individuals, Werther begins to realize the violent implications of his own egoistic project. His language of alterity on the fringes of traditional society is intimately associated with nature as a vision of corporative harmony in the appearance of idyllic permanence, but it is also a discourse on the ethic of manipulative egoism and competitive interaction that undermines the corporative basis of traditional society. Represented as violent nature,

---

[61] "[W]ir nennen das eine Krankheit zum Tode, wodurch die Natur so angegriffen wird, daß ... sie sich nicht ... wiederherzustellen fähig ist." (August 12)

[62] "[I]hn vor meinem Angesicht im Besitz so vieler Vollkommenheiten zu sehen ... hätte mir das Herz zerrissen." (July 30)

this tendency ultimately triumphs. Nature becomes a destructive monster crushing Werther with the power of his own non-corporative aspirations. Fraught with struggle, conflict, and change, the future appears hopeless.

It would be rash to impute to the author of *Werther* a pessimistic view of modern change. Like any modern work, *Werther* articulates many alternative views of contemporary developments. Nevertheless, the projection of what are ultimately historically defined social conflicts, identities, and aspirations as problems of nature raises the aesthetics of the novel to the level of metaphysics. The only solutions proffered by editor and author (in his autobiography) are aesthetic ones — using the novel itself to work through on a personal level the problems discussed in the novel. Disguised as nature and the aesthetics of personal experience, the problems of social isolation facing the new bourgeoisie in the late eighteenth century appear as frightening quandaries that can be at best aesthetically mastered.

The work struck a resonant chord in contemporary audiences, suggesting that its skeptical discussion of change dovetailed with widespread attitudes toward what was happening in contemporary Germany. Since many could identify with Werther's hopes and desires, it seems reasonable to assume that many could also share his hidden terror of nature. In terms of its nature imagery, Goethe's novel articulates both a contemporary fascination with the creative possibilities inherent in Werther's situation and a profound horror of its ultimate implications: the destruction of the old order in the emerging struggle of all against all.

A similar fear can be found in Gerstenberg's *Ugolino*, particularly in its representation of nature as the terrible struggle of isolated individuals among themselves. The work widely acknowledged to have capped the Sturm und Drang movement inaugurated by Gerstenberg's play and continued by Goethe's novel is Friedrich Schiller's *Räuber* (1781). Unlike *Werther*, it features little violent nature imagery, but it does represent wild nature in the form of a forest in which Karl's bandits take refuge. Is this refuge in nature ultimately a realm of hope, or does it lead like Werther's own pursuit of alternative identities in nature to destruction?

5

Nature and History in Schiller's *Räuber*

FRIEDRICH SCHILLER'S PLAY *DIE Räuber* was controversial from the start. In its first staging in 1782, the director Wolfgang Heribert von Dalberg insisted that the play be presented in a fifteenth-century context, since the usurpation and tyranny depicted in it belonged to the past. Supported by most of the cast, Schiller objected to the old-fashioned costumes imposed by Dalberg, complaining that his characters were "lifted from the lap of our present-day world, and were no good in the age of Maximilian."[1] Schiller intended to present contemporary problems in Germany, not those of a distant past. References in the play to the outbreak of the Seven Years' War and to the battlefield death of Prussian Field Marshall Kurt Christoph von Schwerin before Prague identify the play's time period as 1756-1757.[2]

In his preface of 1781, Schiller says his play is designed to provide "a copy of the real world." He disavows the "idealistic affectations" and "constructed characters" that often served as models of virtue and morality in eighteenth-century plays, instead claiming to depict "whole human beings" drawn from nature. Schiller's purpose is to show a slice

---

[1] "...aus dem Schoß unserer Gegenwärtigen Welt herausgehoben, und taugten nichts in dem Maximilianischen Zeitalter." Quoted in Klaus Scherpe, "Friedrich Schiller. Die Räuber," *Dramen des Sturm und Drang* (Stuttgart: Reclam, 1987), 167-168.

[2] Friedrich Schiller, *Die Räuber* (Stuttgart: Reclam, 1969), 48-49. This text, which corresponds to the first edition of the play in 1781, is based on Gerhard Fricke and Herbert G. Göpfert, *Friedrich Schiller, Sämtliche Werke* (Munich: Hanser, 1965). Since all references are from this edition, page numbers appear in parentheses following each footnoted quote.

of contemporary life, inviting the reader to draw his or her own conclusions by measuring "its power against the truth."[3]

What Schiller portrays in his play is a world in utter disarray. "The laws of the world have become a game of chance," Karl declares, "the bond of nature is sundered, the old strife is loose, the son has murdered his father."[4] Franz's intrigues against his father and brother set the plot in motion by breaking the "bond of nature" — natural ties of family devotion. Karl's disinheritance and alienation from his father then provide the motivation for the sequence of events that drives the play to its bloody conclusion. Driven by all that has gone awry in the natural order of things, Karl takes to the woods to form a gang of bandits and wreak vengeance against exploiters and intriguers. Although avenging his father, he fails to restore the old order, finally succumbing to the violence he and his brother unleash.

What exactly are the original bonds of nature, and what sinister workings destroy them? By its very design, Schiller's play projects a certain view of a changing world. The purpose of this chapter is to examine how violent nature imagery in the play intersects with this view of social change.

The Endangered Old Order

The play's opening lines introduce changing times and a past in devolution. "But are you feeling alright, father?" Franz asks. "You look so pale."[5] Franz's feigned solicitude for his father's health meshes with his plan to undermine it with his fabricated letter about Karl. Count von Moor's precarious health immediately becomes evident and remains so until the end, when the old man finally dies after being figuratively buried by one son and literally buried by the other. The survival of a frail

---

[3] Schiller defends his depiction of evil characters in the play. "Jeder Menschenmaler ist in diese Notwendigkeit gesetzt, wenn er anders eine Kopie der wirklichen Welt und keine idealische Affektationen, keine Kompendienmenschen geliefert haben will.... Wer sich den Zweck vorgezeichnet hat, das Laster zu stürzen und Religion, Moral und bürgerliche Gesetze an ihren Feinden zu rächen" must show how "das Laster ... mitsamt seinem ganzen innern Räderwerk" actually works so that the reader can measure "ihre Kraft an der Wahrheit." (3-5)

[4] "Die Gesetze der Welt sind Würfelspiel worden, das Band der Natur ist entzwei, die alte Zwietracht ist los, der Sohn hat seinen Vater erschlagen." (116)

[5] "Aber ist euch wohl, Vater? Ihr seht so blaß aus." (9)

and unhealthy old order identified with Moor — whether the family structure of father and sons or Count and subjects — quickly becomes and remains a central issue throughout the play.

Why does the old order appear so frail? Franz's machinations are designed to undermine his father's health, but Franz capitalizes on a pre-existing situation to do so: Karl's absence from home and his misbehavior while away. "Oh Karl! Karl!" Moor wails. "If only you knew how your behavior tortures the heart of a father! How a single happy bit of news from you would add ten years to my life — would restore my youth — whereas now every report, alas! takes me one step nearer the grave!"[6] These lines introduce a pre-history to the play, suggesting not only past bad news about Karl, but also an earlier time when the family was united and Karl was the joy of a robust father. Karl's alienation from his family (Franz calls him his lost brother) through absence and misbehavior undermines his father's health. Both brothers contribute to the decline of their father and — by extension — to that of the old order.

There is one hope: a single bit of happy news from Karl could save his father. The old order could live on through Karl if only news of his reformation would restore it. At issue is an ideal mode of behavior and set of relations that appear corrupted, but could still be restored.

In Scene 2 of Act I, Karl renounces his previous defiance of his father and vows to return home. "In the shade of my father's groves," he declares, "in the arms of my Amalia a noble delight beckons me."[7] This cryptic statement identifies the old order with idyllic nature space in the shade of groves offering a sense of cyclical renewal and continuity in association with family tradition and sexual reproduction. It offers security in the shelter of home and family from vague dangers in the outside world, and it is situated in the past, a paradise lost to Karl, who never recovers it.

The idyllic character of the old order emerges in various images: garden scenes (the door to the garden frequented by Amalia offers the promise of conjugal bliss with her and renewal of the family circle), the picturesque region Karl surveys from a hill under trees with sunset behind the Danube (where Karl remembers his childhood and dreams

---

[6] "O Karl! Karl! Wüßtest du, wie deine Aufführung das Vaterherz foltert! Wie eine einzige frohe Nachricht von dir meinem Leben zehen Jahre zusetzen würde - mich zum Jüngling machen würde - da mich nun jede, ach! - einen Schritt näher ans Grab rückt!" (9)

[7] "Im Schatten meiner väterlichen Haine, in den Armen meiner Amalia lockt mich ein edler Vergnügen." (28)

of "the whole world one family and one father there up above"),[8] and the rural area around the Moor palace where Karl experiences the feeling of coming home. This last image associates home and family with the countryside. Its lowlands, hills, streams, woods, and mountains all exude "a balsam of ecstasy" in "elysium," promising security in paradise to "the poor refugee" Karl. The vague dangers Karl flees from are implicitly associated with city life.

Karl experiences coming home as a process of focusing in from broad expanses of unfettered nature (hills, streams, and forests) to sheltered corners in enclosed areas. "See there also the swallow nests in the palace courtyard," he continues, "also the garden door! — and this corner in the fence."[9] The nests, courtyard, garden door, and fence corner Karl identifies with home signify enclosed, utilized nature spaces. Notably, they are associated with a history of conquest and domination: "and down there the meadow valley where you, the hero Alexander, ... defeated the Persian satrap."[10] Home is comprised of secure borders protected from a menacing outside world by walls within which a military tradition and an established history of domination and subordination flourish. An outside world of change and uncertainty implicitly associated with city life is excluded by the secure walls and idyllic nature terrain of home.

Home is also the site of the intimate family circle. "As an exalted father I made my way among the fathers of the people," Moor recalls. "My children blossomed full of hope beautifully around me."[11] Family is defined less by blood relation than by feelings of intimacy, bringing Moor to include his niece Amalia within the family circle as his daughter, a designation that anticipates her expected marriage to Karl. The intimate family circle securely harbored at home functions to reproduce itself in a ceaseless cycle. "Here you were supposed to once lead your life," Karl tells himself, "a tall, handsome, admired man — here live your boyhood years for the second time in Amalia's thriving children — here!

---

[8] "[D]ie ganze Welt *eine* Familie und ein Vater dort oben..." (81)

[9] "Sieh da auch die Schwalbennester im Schloßhof, auch das Gartentürchen! - und diese Ecke am Zaun." (89)

[10] "...und dort unten das Wiesental, wo du, der Held Alexander ... den persischen Satrapen niederwarfst." (89)

[11] "Ein gepriesener Vater ging ich einher unter den Vätern der Menschen," Moor recalls. "Schön um mich blühten meine Kinder voll Hoffnung." (131)

the idol of your people."[12] Karl envisions a traditional course of events interrupted by his alienation from home and family: he would have returned to the past to relive his childhood had he married Amalia and had children. The family ideal of the old order is circular and cyclical in patterns designed to exclude difference, distance, and change in the outside world.

Like Karl, his father longs to see him return home and continue the old order. His dream — articulated in the first scene by Franz — is to see Karl assume dominion over his territory after him and rule in the same benevolent spirit of service to the state, a tradition seven centuries old. The original Count von Moor served Emperor Frederick I against pirates and was raised by him to the nobility and, implicitly, installed as count. Since counts were originally instated by the Salian and Ottonian emperors to administer imperial territory in service to the state, and since Frederick I tried to reassert the tradition of imperial authority in Germany, this bit of Moor family history serves to highlight an important point: the ideal order to which Karl aspires to return home is predicated on serving the state and territorial prince. The authority of family father and territorial ruler go hand in hand. "My father," Franz recalls, "changed his territory into a family circle, sat sweetly smiling at the gate, and greeted [his subjects] as brothers and children."[13] The language of territorial dominion blends with that of patriarchal authority within the family.

A key element of the old order is its harmony among the hierarchically structured estates. Until it is sabotaged by Franz, there is no semblance of conflict or competing aspirations in the family circle of loyal subjects and protective ruler. The aristocrat Kosinsky's betrothal to someone of bourgeois background and Karl's virtual engagement to Amalia, who stems from the lower nobility, imply a harmony of interests superseding and reconciling differences among the estates. The Moor family tradition of loyal service to and reward from the emperor highlights a harmony of interests in the old order between nobility and king or emperor, as does the fiction of Karl's serving King Frederick II of Prussia in the military. Despite this family spirit of harmony and reconciliation among the estates, the lines of authority remain clearly drawn: as "idol of his people," the ruler expects to be worshipped and obeyed without question.

---

[12] "Hier solltest du wandeln dereinst, ein großer, stattlicher, gepriesener Mann - hier dein Knabenleben in Amalias blühenden Kindern zum zweiten Mal leben - hier! der Abgott deines Volks." (89)

[13] "Mein Vater schuf sein Gebiet zu einem Familienzirkel um, saß liebreich lächelnd am Tor, und grüßte sie Brüder und Kinder." (54)

The language of idyllic nature blends with that of home and family to produce a utopian vision of corporative harmony under the benevolent rule of the territorial prince. The sense of refuge and homecoming central to this vision is predicated on restoring continuity with the past in a way that obviates change. In the old order, the intimate family circle functions to reproduce itself in a ceaseless cycle of new faces and old ways. The idyllic "paradise lost" of the old order, its circularity and cyclical character, the insular way in which it delimits nature space by bordering off and protecting from outside influences, and its social representation of harmonious hierarchy all suggest an underlying abhorrence of conflict and change. Yet something happens to end Karl's golden childhood years while frustrating Moor's golden dreams of perpetuity, destroying the old order and transforming it into memory.

The Rise of Tyranny

The third edition of the play (1799) by Tobias Löffler emphasizes the importance of the tyranny theme in the play by placing the words *in Tirannos* on the title page. The machinations of tyranny are developed in the play by Franz, whose schemes ruin the hopes and dreams of his father and brother. What motivates Franz? Why does he plot to sabotage any hope of restoring the old order?

"I have much right," Franz claims, "to be displeased with nature."[14] Nature has done him the disservice of giving him an older brother, depriving him of an inheritance under the laws of primogeniture. Franz rebels against the notion that one's social status is fixed at birth. "Who gave [nature] the power," he demands, "to bestow this to him and keep it from me?"[15] Of course, the problem Franz addresses is not natural, but social — the disinheritance of younger sons of the aristocracy. Still, the old order is equated with nature even by those who question it.

Refusing to accept the notion that the advantages of birth and station are bestowed by nature, Franz redefines nature in a more modern, almost Darwinian sense. "No! no!" he declares,

> I do [nature] an injustice. It imparted to us the spirit of invention, set us naked and impoverished on the shore of this great ocean world — Swim whoever can swim, and whoever is too

---

[14] "Ich habe große Rechte, über die Natur ungehalten zu sein." (16)

[15] "Wer hat [der Natur] die Vollmacht gegeben, jenem dieses zu verleihen und mir vorzuenthalten?" (16)

clumsy, sink! It imparted nothing to me; whatever I want to make of myself is up to me. Everybody has the same right to the greatest and least of things, claim is destroyed by claim, drive by drive, and power by power. Right resides with the vanquisher, and the limits of our power are our laws.[16]

Franz's credo defies the traditional belief in a God-given natural order that predetermines one's lot in life. All are equally entitled to whatever they can get, no matter what station they are born into. The only limiting factor is individual ability and enterprise. Nature is a violent struggle of all against all for survival and supremacy, a concept of nature that dovetails with Franz's ethic of self-interest.

In Franz's system of individual enterprise, the altruism and morality of the old order give way to the logic of the pocketbook. "Of course, there are certain communal pacts entered into in order to govern the pulses of the world cycle," Franz acknowledges. "Honest name! Truly a rich coin with which one can barter brilliantly. ... Conscience ... that too a well-written bill of exchange with which the bankrupt can in a pinch still make do."[17] The trademarks of honor and morality are commodities to be cashed in exchange for the ability to dominate others. The social conventions that organize society by birth and station give way to new organizing principles of the marketplace: exchange value now controls the pulse of the world.

In order to assert a sovereign sense of self, Franz defies the old order, liberating himself from a system that defines individual worth in terms of factors over which the individual has no control. "Can I recognize a love," he argues, "that is not based on regard for my self?"[18] Such arguments, which define individual worth in terms of what the

---

[16] "Nein! nein! Ich tu [der Natur] Unrecht. Gab sie uns doch Erfindungsgeist mit, setzte uns nackt und armselig ans Ufer dieses großen Ozeans Welt - Schwimme, wer schwimmen kann, und wer zu plump ist, geh unter! Sie gab mir nichts mit; wozu ich mich machen will, das ist nun meine Sache. Jeder hat gleiches Recht zum Größten und Kleinsten, Anspruch wird an Anspruch, Trieb an Trieb und Kraft an Kraft zernichtet. Das Recht wohnet beim Überwältiger, und die Schranken unserer Kraft sind unsere Gesetze." (17)

[17] "Wohl gibt es gewisse gemeinschaftliche Pakta, die man geschlossen hat, die Pulse des Weltzirkels zu treiben. Ehrlicher Name! Wahrhaftig, eine reichhaltige Münze, mit der sich meisterlich schachern läßt ... Gewissen ... auch das ein gut geschriebener Wechselbrief mit dem auch der Bankerottierer zur Not noch hinauslangt." (17)

[18] "Kann ich eine Liebe erkennen, die sich nicht auf Achtung gegen mein Selbst gründet?" (18)

individual is or does rather than accident of birth, carry an emancipatory moment undermining the old order.

They also inflate the value of the ego above all else. Franz's self-emancipation leads to his self-aggrandizement at the expense of others. "I will eradicate everything around me that keeps me from being master," he declares.[19] Franz's credo of violent struggle for mastery of all against all anticipates the principle of the free market under laissez-faire capitalism, and the author's implicit condemnation of it amounts to an early critique of the capitalist ethic incipient in the new bourgeoisie.

It is a conservative critique. Tyranny is identified not with oppressive structures of absolutism in corporative society, but with the emancipatory forces of individualism that were undermining them. By liberating himself and usurping dominion from his father, Franz demonstrates in the play itself that history is no longer a cyclical sequence of events reaffirming the old order, but a dynamic process of conflict and confrontation among antagonistic interests. The play's defense of the traditional order against Franz's system suggests revulsion toward processes of change and a nostalgic wish to return home to a mythical time of stability and harmony under a benevolent central authority.

Franz is not the only one at odds with the old order. While the letter he reads his father about his brother Karl's outrageous behavior may be fraudulent, it is essentially true: Karl has frittered away his time and money in Leipzig with drinking, gambling, and student pranks. Deeply in debt, he and his comrades arrive at a tavern on Saxony's borders as refugees from the law.

The tavern's border location poses a problem for Karl and his comrades. They must choose between returning to Leipzig to face the consequences of their debts; going home to the idyllic countryside of Franconia with its paternal groves, an option open to Karl; or entering the Bohemian forests of banditry. These options are associated with urban life, the agrarian countryside, and the wild woods respectively. Each setting is demarcated by borders that are not only regional, but political: Saxony, Franconia (under Bavaria), and Bohemia (under the Hapsburgs) form separate dominions, with the tavern located where their borders meet. City, countryside, and wild nature are represented as mutually exclusive territories offering radically different choices in life.

The city is quickly excluded from consideration. Returning would mean the hardships of prison, hard labor, or military service. For his

---

[19] "Ich will alles um mich her ausrotten, was mich einschränkt, daß ich nicht Herr bin." (18)

part, Karl rejects the city's corruption. "There they stifle healthy nature with tasteless conventions," he observes,

> kiss up to the shoe shiner so that he mentions them to His Lordship and mistreat the poor rascal whom they don't fear. — Deify each other for a midday meal and would like to poison each other over a mattress for which they are outbid. ... Faint when they see a goose bleed, and clap their hands when their neighbor leaves the stock exchange bankrupt. — No matter how warmly I shook their hands: — Just one more day! — In vain! — into the slammer with the scum![20]

The activities Karl berates here all occur in public. Whether the prince's servants are being flattered, a bed auctioned, or a goose slaughtered, it takes place outside the home in the streets, shops, markets, or before the halls of power. Taken together in their various functions, these locations define a sphere of public activity as opposed to the private sphere of the intimate family circle located in the Franconian countryside.

The public sphere perverts nature: there is no human sympathy among Karl's debtors with his pleas for clemency. Feelings of empathy and intimacy cultivated in private are displaced in public by a pervasive obsession with driving one's competitor bankrupt. The state enforces laws tailored to the needs of both marketplace and prince, and the townspeople turn a profit by fawning before authority. "They fortify themselves in the stomach lining of a tyrant," Karl observes, "cater to the moods of his stomach and let themselves be pressured by his flatulence."[21] Political tyranny is linked to the incipient spirit of private enterprise in Germany's cities.

Karl, who has already broken the rules of the marketplace by defaulting on his debts, now declares war on the state. "Place me before an army of fellows like me, and Germany will become a republic to make

---

[20] "Da verrammeln sie sich die gesunde Natur mit abgeschmackten Konventionen, belecken den Schuhputzer, daß er sie vertrete bei Ihro Gnaden, und hudeln den armen Schelm, den sie nicht fürchten. — Vergöttern sich um ein Mittagessen und möchten einander vergiften um ein Unterbett, das ihnen beim Aufstreich überboten wird. ... Fallen in Ohnmacht, wenn sie eine Gans bluten sehen, und klatschen in die Hände, wenn ihr Nebenbuhler bankerott von der Börse geht. — So warm ich ihnen die Hand drückte: — Nur noch einen Tag! — Umsonst! — ins Loch mit dem Hund!"

[21] "Sie verpalisadieren sich ins Baufell eines Tyrannen, hofieren der Laune seines Magens und lassen sich klemmen von seinen Winden." (20)

Rome and Sparta look like convents."[22] Something like this happens when Karl becomes bandit chieftain, but the result is hardly a republic. Karl takes absolute charge. His autocratic rule suits his military-aristocratic background, but not his stated republican ends, and the republican issue is never revived. Spiegelberg's revolt against Karl's autocracy in the name of freedom is represented as a corrupt power grab, while Schweizer's unquestioning subservience appears noble. While a powerful critique of tyranny pervades the play, democracy is scarcely the proffered alternative.

Karl uses a rhetorical technique to illustrate the republic he has in mind: Rome and Sparta would be convents by comparison. Sparta was known to Schiller's contemporaries more for its authoritarian exploitation of helots than its republicanism. "Oh! the one-sided freedom that allows its subjects to be serfs," Friedrich Nicolai wrote of Ulm during his travels. "Ulm is no Sparta that it should have to have helots!"[23] In Rome, with its thriving slavery, the republic was ultimately crushed in a sequence of events alluded to in the play's passage on Caesar and Brutus in Act IV. Comparing a German republic to Rome and Sparta, both of which ultimately dispensed with republican freedoms, seems odd.

The reference to convents may help explain the comparison. If Karl would make Germany so republican that Rome and Sparta would be convents by comparison, then a republic must be the opposite of a convent. Convents were peaceful, orderly retreats from worldly affairs, often in the countryside, in which each member had certain prescribed duties and privileges, much like the family circle surrounding Moor's palace in Franconia. Like Rome and Sparta, with their authoritarian traditions of bloody conquest and brutal subjugation, a republic must be the opposite of this vision of peaceful corporative harmony.

In this context, Karl's call for a republic challenges the very basis of the old order represented by his father. Karl would lead an army of men like himself against an idealized imperial dominion served for seven centuries by generations of Moors. Citing the historical models of Rome and Sparta, Karl implicitly embraces their martial histories. He would bring about conflict and change through conquest at the expense of the prized cyclical continuity of the old order. When he unwittingly unleash-

---

[22] "Stelle mich vor ein Heer Kerls wie ich, und aus Deutschland soll eine Republik werden, gegen die Rom und Sparta Nonnenklöster sein sollen." (20)

[23] "O! der einseitigen Freyheit, welche ihre Unterthanen leibeigen seyn läßt. Ulm ist doch kein Sparta, daß es Heloten haben müßte!" Quoted in Horst Moeller, *Fürstenstaat oder Bürgernation? Deutschland 1763-1815* (Berlin: Siedler Verlag, 1989), 138.

es Spiegelberg and his band against the convent they pillage and burn (prefiguring his own gang's sacking of the Moor palace), Karl demolishes the very thing he would preserve, the healthy nature he defends. His call for a republic that would render Rome and Sparta convents by comparison undermines its own premise.

Of course, Karl's call for a republic also criticizes the public corruption he witnesses in the city, but his alternative, like the models of Rome and Sparta he invokes, appears fatally flawed. It plunges him into an inextricable predicament: if he struggles for freedom from public corruption, he must violently confront it in public; yet doing so would violate the ideals of harmony and cyclical continuity in the private sphere that were corrupted to begin with. If the intimate family circle in the Franconian countryside offers a cyclical permanence of life in a whole and harmonious natural order, and if the public sphere corrupts that order by fomenting conflict among competing interests, then Karl also perverts it by challenging public authority and forcibly assuming the mantle of absolute authority himself.

Karl was already involved in similar episodes in Leipzig, including one described by Spiegelberg. In order to avenge harm done to his dog by faculty members at the university, Karl corners the market on meat and proclaims a city-wide fast. When the magistracy and wealthier citizenry plot revenge, Karl leads students and guilds into the streets, threatening to sack the city. He uses market mechanisms and social organizing to bring festering social conflicts among disparate sectors (students and administrators, artisans and patricians) into the open in order to avenge an injustice by the authorities. His participation in public controversy and conflict undermines the corporative ideal of harmonious hierarchy represented by his father.

However, in the tavern on the Saxon border, Karl can still escape his quandary by returning to the privacy of home and family. He vows to appeal to Moor for forgiveness, expecting fatherly sympathy. He seeks the human compassion missing from the public sphere in the idyllic country setting of the intimate family circle.

Instead, he finds that the family circle itself has been corrupted. Moor's willingness to allow himself to be manipulated and Karl's own gullibility permit Franz to transform the Moor palace from a refuge of humanity into a prison designed to dehumanize its inmates: Franz promises that if Karl returns he will be kept in the dungeon until "your hair grows like eagle feathers and your nails like bird claws."[24] Ironi-

---

[24] "...bis deine Haare wachsen wie Adlersfedern und deine Nägel wie Vogelsklauen." (26)

cally, Franz's otherwise deceptive letter is straightforward in this regard, disillusioning Karl about the possibility of going home. "What a fool I was to want to return to the cage!" he declares.[25] The secure, protective borders and walls of home and family are transformed by both brothers into prison bars, and Karl renounces the private sphere forever with the words, "I no longer have a father, no longer a love."[26]

Karl raises his failure to find compassion at home to cosmic proportions. "Lions and leopards feed their young, crows put carrion on the table for their little ones, and He, He..."[27] Since all of nature nurtures its offspring in time of need, Moor's failure to do so violates the natural order, and Karl calls on nature to avenge itself. "I want to be a bear and incite the bears of the North against this murderous race," he intones, "...I wish I could blow the trumpet of revolt throughout nature [and] lead air, earth, and sea into battle against this hyena brood!"[28] As the shelter of home turns into prison, the surrounding idyllic nature terrain becomes violent with the impending family power struggle. Behind the facade of family intimacy lurks the reality of isolation and competitive conflict corrupting the ideal old order.

Karl decides to join the bandits in the woods in order to avenge a violated natural order. At this point, the third option open to Karl at the tavern — the Bohemian forests — intersects with the first: in both the forests of banditry and the city of Leipzig, Karl shares in the corruption of the authorities by publicly punishing it. The Bohemian woods have in common with the Franconian countryside of home and family their nature terrain: both offer alternatives to the corruption of city life. However, the forests of banditry pervert nature in sharing in the violent confrontation and competitive conflict that corrupt the public sphere. Who are the bandits, and how do their activities pervert the old order of corporative harmony while avenging it?

---

[25] "[W]as für ein Tor ich war, daß ich ins Käficht zurückwollte!" (33)

[26] "Ich habe keinen Vater mehr, ich habe keine Liebe mehr." (33)

[27] "Löwen und Leoparden füttern ihre Jungen, Raben tischen ihren Kleinen auf dem Aas, und Er, Er..." (31)

[28] "Ich möchte ein Bär sein, und die Bären des Nordlands wider dies mörderische Geschlecht anhetzen, ... daß ich durch die ganze Natur das Horn des Aufruhrs blasen könnte, Luft, Erde und Meer wider das Hyänengezücht ins Treffen zu führen!" (31, 32)

The Forests of Banditry

The bandits in the play are diverse in origin and motivation. The core group (Spiegelberg, Schweizer, Roller, and Karl's other Leipzig comrades) is comprised of student libertines of limited means from modest backgrounds. Eighteenth-century students in Germany often came from relatively poor homes and relied on state subsidies and private charity to survive. Their prospects were bleak. Roller mentions founding an almanac and writing literary commentary for a few pennies. Schufterle thinks of becoming a Pietist and offering weekly tutorials. Grimm would become an atheist and have his books banned and burned, Razmann a physician and pharmacist. Typically, German university graduates from poor backgrounds were lucky to find placement as rural curates and school teachers dependent on the charity of their impoverished parishioners, or struggled to survive as literary critics persecuted for unorthodox writings, or made a modest living in the medical profession.[29] Often they were fated to lives of squalor and low esteem. Already threatened with debtor's prison, and with few prospects anyway if they return to city life, Karl's comrades turn to banditry.

Spiegelberg recruits a second group of bandits, ruined shopkeepers and unemployed scholars and clerks from Suabia. This group alludes to social misery in the author's homeland. Petty merchants were being ruined by competition as well as by taxation and state restrictions designed to favor new enterprises more capable of paying into state coffers.[30] The state subsidized the education of more young men than the civil service could accommodate. Those ruined by state mercantilistic and educational policies found themselves economically and socially isolated from the corporative mainstream. With little to lose, in Schiller's play they join the outlaws.

There is a third type of bandit — Karl and his admirer Kosinsky. Both are disinherited aristocrats deprived of opportunity by corruption and tyranny. In the eighteenth century, sons of the nobility disinherited by primogeniture or otherwise in trouble often had little recourse beyond the military, where positions as officers were usually reserved for them. Since the natural order of things has been reversed for Karl by his brother's usurpation and his father's refusal to help him, he naturally takes to the woods to become a bandit chieftain.

---

[29] Bruford, 250-263.

[30] Brunschwig, 104-105, 112.

Whatever their background, the bandits are all isolated from the mainstream of corporative society. As would-be civil servants and professionals, most originally aspired to join the new bourgeoisie on the fringes of corporative society. Only Karl and Kosinsky clearly belonged to a traditional estate. The course of events places both beyond the pale: Karl renounces his seemingly corrupted heritage, while Kosinsky's murder of his bride's seducer makes him an outlaw. Like the others, both have lost a stake in a traditional order that no longer guarantees them social and economic stability and security. In one way or another, Schiller's bandits are all alienated from traditional corporative roles.

This alienation is reflected in the bandits' non-corporative aspirations and values. Spiegelberg best represents the spirit of individual enterprise. He refuses to follow anyone else, claiming the right to lead the bandits. It was his idea to form the bandit gang to begin with, and he places a proprietary claim to its leadership, accusing Karl of usurping his right of authorship. He accuses the others of slavish deference and cowardice for electing Karl captain, implying that they are bowing to Karl's aristocratic background instead of recognizing his own superior talents. He quits to start another bandit enterprise with nothing but a staff and returns a self-made man with a notorious corps of seventy-eight followers.

Spiegelberg's entrepreneurial spirit is inspired by a desire to realize his full personal potential ("the most in one person," as he puts it). Barred by social obstacles (including his Jewish heritage) from success, he chooses to pursue fame through notoriety as bandit chieftain. Spiegelberg dreams of historical accomplishments that prove his worth, making him the equal of generals, physicians, and statesmen. "And Spiegelberg they will say in east and west," he predicts.[31] In a system that reserves top posts in the military and bureaucracy for the aristocracy, Spiegelberg's dreams are subversive: he would replace corporative privilege with an ethic of achievement so radical that even superlative bandits are revered. Like Franz, Spiegelberg is eager to make something of himself rather than accept a naturally subordinate lot in life determined by birth and station. Perversely yet poignantly, he articulates the emancipatory aspirations of the new bourgeoisie.

Yet Spiegelberg pursues his aspirations by ruthlessly exploiting others. He manipulates his followers into joining him by ruining their lives and reputations, he pillages a convent, and he plots to murder Karl. His obsession with his own reputation appears thoroughly corrupt, leading to a vain self-obsession that demolishes its legitimacy. Represent-

---

[31] "Und Spiegelberg wird es heißen in Osten und Westen." (24)

ed as immoral and pathetically self-centered, Spiegelberg's incipient spirit of private enterprise offers nothing but trouble. Spread to Karl, who adopts Spiegelberg's idea of banditry, it undermines the old order by corrupting its members. "You didn't draw that from out of your human soul!" Karl tells Schwarz when he first hears of Spiegelberg's banditry proposal, implying the idea's devilish origins.[32]

Karl's role as a bandit sharply contrasts with Spiegelberg's. While Spiegelberg robs for the sake of notoriety, Karl's motive is revenge. As an outlaw, he avenges injustice, and therefore serving under him is no dishonor. Like the mythical Robin Hood, he takes from the rich and gives to the poor, yet he mocks the Robin Hood tradition. For Karl, there is no fame or honor in banditry, nor is money of concern to him. His share of the loot goes almost incidentally to poor children in a conventionally philanthropic manner.

Not honor or compassion, but vengeance is the driving force behind Karl's banditry. "Revenge is my trade," he declares.[33] Karl's victims include aristocratic landowners, officers, a count and his lawyer, a minister, and a government official. However, he stops short of attacking a prince, the ultimate authority under absolutism, and Kosinsky murders the minister who abducts his bride rather than the prince who actually seduces her. Despite its anti-authoritarian thrust, banditry in the play retains a latent reverence for corporative authority. Corruption is rooted not in the corporative system, but in wicked parvenus who finagle their way into a prince's favor, or in a few aristocrats misguided by lawyers and greed.

The transgressions Karl punishes are rooted not in the corporative system, but in modern change. For instance, Karl attacks landowners for exploiting their peasants. Since the fifteenth century, this abuse had usually taken the form of increasing seignorial demands for payment and services, demands successful enough to be have been branded the second wave of feudal bondage.[34] The sine qua non of these demands was the spread of a money economy and the availability of new luxury items for a price. The aristocracy found itself increasingly compelled to accumulate money in order to maintain its status and lifestyle, and its

---

[32] "Das hast du nicht aus deiner Menschenseele hervorgeholt!" (34)

[33] "Rache ist mein Gewerbe." (73)

[34] Hans Mottek calls it "die zweite Leibeigenschaft." The first wave of feudal bondage occurred in the early Middle Ages. Hans Mottek, *Wirtschaftsgeschichte Deutschlands* (Berlin: VEB Deutscher Verlag der Wissenschaften, 1973), I, 234-240.

chief source of income was the wealth produced by peasants (whether as serfs or tenants) on its estates. By the eighteenth century, a flourishing money economy led to peasant exploitation on a perhaps unprecedented scale, except where the state (interested in preserving its tax base) protected the peasantry. When Karl directs his wrath against landowners able to mercilessly exploit their subjects, he is scarcely attacking the system of peasant exploitation itself, but rather its excesses due to the modern influence of a money economy.

Karl also punishes a minister for ruining others in order to advance his own career. The minister's transgression is his egoistic pursuit of his own interests at the expense of others, the fundamental ethic of capitalism. The government official Karl targets infused market relations into his ministry by selling posts, while the count and his lawyer made a mockery of justice by unfairly winning a suit worth "a million." Like an officer who misused the laws and bought off the judiciary, they corrupted justice for profit. Karl's vengeance is directed against spreading market relations and a concomitant ethic of competition and profiteering characteristic not of traditional corporative relations, but of the incipient market economy that undermines them. The problem is not the old order, but its displacement by the new entrepreneurial spirit of modernity.

Paradoxically, Karl displays the same egoistic preoccupation with his own interests he condemns in others. Before taking to the woods, he shows little interest in social injustice except when it affects him personally (in the Leipzig episode when his dog was killed). His vengeful mission starts when his father denies him succor in time of need. Whenever Karl punishes social injustice, he vicariously avenges this injustice to himself. There is an egoistic basis to his banditry: he callously uses others to avenge an imagined slight to himself, turning them into instruments or victims for his own selfish purpose. He assumes sole authority to judge and execute the corrupt by virtue of the summary justice he exercises through his gang of bandits, and he dares the authorities to judge him for thus imitating their own corruption. The bandits themselves are merely "miserable instruments of my larger plans, like the noose contemptibly in the hand of the hangman."[35]

When the knot of family intrigue unravels at the play's end, Karl abruptly abandons his campaign against tyranny. He is ready to desert the bandits and his cause as soon as Amalia forgives him. In restoring the intimate family circle, the prodigal son would figuratively return

---

[35] "...[e]lende Werkzeuge meiner größeren Plane, wie der Strick verächtlich in der Hand des Henkers." (74)

home to his father. Karl's own unhappiness is ultimately all that matters to him.

Karl's self-preoccupation alienates him from his fellow bandits. While they revel in the adventure and booty of banditry on the banks of the Danube, he mourns his lost family ties. "I alone the outcast," he laments, "...for me no longer the sweet name child — never again the lover's languishing gaze — never ever again the bosom friend's embrace!"[36] Karl is hardly the only outcast; none of the bandits have any hope of family intimacy, either. However, they not only have no desire for it, they are unable to understand why anyone would. Unable to fathom Karl's remorse for the lost opportunities of childhood, or his nostalgic association of the picturesque region along the Danube with the old order, they have forfeited their last shred of humanity — conscience and a lost sense of family intimacy. Karl sees himself as all alone, "surrounded by murderers — by hissing vipers."[37] In the world of banditry, Karl corrupts the old order of corporative and family harmony in much the same way as the public officials he punishes: preoccupied with his own designs and interests, Karl reifies his fellows as instruments or dehumanizes them as vipers, a reference to the serpent Satan and a nature gone bad. This leaves him alone, isolated even from his fellow outsiders. In the Bohemian forests, the new order displaces the old corporative harmony as much as it does in the urban seats of power.

In using the bandits as instruments, Karl shares his brother Franz's tyrannical proclivities. Karl promises that the bandit who "burns in the wildest way, murders in the most horrible ... shall be royally rewarded."[38] Yet when Schufterle brags about throwing an infant into the flames during the bandit raid on Nuremberg, Karl arbitrarily banishes him from the gang. This amounts to a death sentence, since expulsion from the gang means vulnerability to capture and execution, and Schufterle soon hangs. "You wonder about it?" Karl challenges the rest of the bandits, who are appalled by the measure's harshness. "Who

---

[36] "Ich allein der Verstoßene, ... mir nicht der süße Name Kind — nimmer mir der Geliebten schmachtender Blick — nimmer des Busenfreundes Umarmung!" (81-82)

[37] "Umlagert von Mördern — von Nattern umzischt" (82)

[38] "am wildesten sengt, am gräßlichsten mordet ... soll königlich belohnt werden..." (33)

wonders where I command?"³⁹ The arbitrary and unjust control Karl exercises over his fellow bandits verges on tyranny.

Karl's bandit role as avenger of a disturbed natural order culminates in his attack on Franz's palace. He vows before nature itself to avenge its violation by Franz, calling his bandits "the arm of higher majesties" and "terrible angels of [God's] dark judgment."⁴⁰ Yet in avenging his father, Karl violates the very family ties he avenges. "I hereby sunder from now on for all time the fraternal tie," he declares. "I hereby damn every drop of fraternal blood before the face of the open heaven!"⁴¹ Renouncing his brother is like his earlier renunciation of father and love: both vows destroy the natural bonds uniting the intimate family circle. Karl's punishment of Franz for violating family ties violates those ties itself.

This contradiction in Karl's role as bandit avenger is mirrored in other venues. In punishing tyranny, he exercises tyrannical authority. In attacking public officials corrupted by self-interest, he is motivated by preoccupation with his own fate. He uses others as instruments in order to avenge the instrumentalization of others. And he indulges in the market relations that foment the ethic of competitive egoism undermining the old order.

In choosing banditry in the Bohemian forests over returning home to his father or to city life in Leipzig, Karl opts for an alternative lifestyle in a life-and-death struggle with a corrupt public order. The open, untamed forests allow him to develop an individual identity in opposition to the public sphere. At the same time, however, his very entanglement with public officials in perennial conflict taints him with their corruption. Locked in conflict with the authorities, Karl embraces the very values he combats. The remembered idyllic terrain of home and family gives way to nature's violence in a world turned upside down in the woods.

The Nemesis of Violent Nature

---

³⁹ "Überlegt ihr? Wer überlegt, wann ich befehle?" (67)

⁴⁰ Karl vows that if he fails to avenge his father, "so speie die Natur mich aus ihren Grenzen wie eine bösartige Bestie aus." "Das hat euch wohl niemals geträumet daß ihr der Arm höherer Majestäten seid?" he inquires, asking his bandits to pray to the one "der euch gewürdiget hat, die schröcklichen Engel seines finstern Gerichtes zu sein!" (117)

⁴¹ "So zerreiß ich von nun an auf ewig das brüderliche Band. So verfluch ich jeden Tropfen brüderlichen Bluts im Antlitz des offenen Himmels!" (116)

Schiller's play represents two worlds in conflict: the private sphere of the intimate family circle and the public sphere of official corruption. What unites the two are Franz and Karl, who start out in the private sphere and eventually assume roles with public implications, Franz in control of his father's domain and Karl as bandit chieftain. The play shows the history of Moor family devolution as its characters move from the private sphere out into public. The precarious health of the old order at the play's outset — associated private sphere intimacy — is shattered by its end.

This historical theme has two dimensions. The first dimension is continuity or tradition, associated with the idea of the old order. Moor's emphasis on his reputation and the portrait gallery of Moor ancestors invoke 700 years of Moor family tradition. When Karl and Amalia as potential spouses and parents contemplate the portraits together, they symbolize the hope of continuing the old order in the present. However, after years away in the city and forests of banditry, Karl appears unrecognizable. His alienation from Amalia prevents re-membering the past of family intimacy and corporative harmony.

The theme of returning home by remembering it is intimately associated with idyllic nature imagery. On the banks of the Danube, Karl reflects on the harvest cycle ("the grapevine full of hope"), then recalls his childhood; and in the garden at the Moor palace, Amalia remembers scenes of love with Karl. "It seemed to me as if nature rejuvenated itself," she declares.[42] The cyclical continuity of the old order finds expression in memories evoked by nature's secure, ceaseless cycles.

However, nature also has a foreboding dimension associated with change or historical discontinuity. "But overnight hail could fall," Karl observes of the harvest along the Danube, "and destroy it all."[43] This consideration leads Karl to melancholy reflections about his lost home and family, and he calls on nature to mourn their loss. "He sails on stormy seas," Amalia says of her missing lover, "...he travels through uncharted sandy deserts ... the midday scorches his bare head, northern snow shrinks the souls of his feet, stormy hail rains around his temples."[44] Symbolized by the wild and violent nature imagery Amalia

---

[42] "Mir wars, als ob die Natur sich verjüngete." (102)

[43] "Aber es kann ja über Nacht ein Hagel fallen und alles zugrund schlagen." (80)

[44] "Er segelt auf ungestümen Meeren ... er wandelt durch ungebahnte, sandigte Wüsten ... der Mittag sengt sein entblößtes Haupt, nordischer Schnee schrumpft seine Sohlen zusammen, stürmischer Hagel regnet um seine Schläfe." (104)

invokes, Karl's wanderings far from home destroy the hope of home and family. Violent nature imagery signals the loss of a patriarchal ideal associated with idyllic nature and its replacement by a new order of conflict and alienation.

The bandits too are associated with both violent nature and historical change. "The forest is our night quarters," they sing, "we work in storm and wind, the moon is our sun."[45] The bandits live in a world turned upside down, where the moon becomes their sun, the forest their home, and a violent storm optimal working weather. Sung against a backdrop of castle ruins, these verses suggest changing times, a perversion of old ways and of nature itself under a new order. As bandit chieftain, Karl subverts the Moor family tradition of serving the state against pirates, news of which literally kills his father, destroying any possible rapprochement. In what may be a parody of Voltaire's Pangloss, Spiegelberg argues that the bandits are historical instruments of divine Providence, since their victims are spared the miseries of war, plague, and medical treatment.[46] In Karl's hand, they become "the sword of vengeance of higher tribunals." "Don't listen to them, avenger in heaven!" Karl intones when the bandits brag of murdering the innocent. "...How can you help it when your pestilence, your inflation, your floods consume the just with the villain?"[47]

As historical agents, the bandits are identified with a nature turned violent and destructive in divine punishment of temporal sin. "We will fall upon them like the Great Flood and fire down at their heads like sheet lightning," Schweizer declares before battle.[48] As Great Flood, the bandits' purpose through Karl is to avenge nature's corruption in the name of a higher order. "Oh unfathomable finger of a vengeful nemesis!" Karl exclaims after Schweizer murders Spiegelberg. "Wasn't it he who sang me the siren song? — Consecrate this knife to the dark

---

[45] "Der Wald ist unser Nachtquartier, Bei Sturm und Wind hantieren wir, Der Mond ist unsre Sonne." (105)

[46] The bandits are "ein würdiges Werkzeug in der Hand der Vorsehung" for relieving "den lieben Gott von manchem lästigen Kostgänger..., ihm Krieg, Pestilenz, teure Zeit und Dokters ersparen." (29)

[47] "Höre sie nicht, Rächer im Himmel! ... Was kannst du dafür, wenn deine Pestilenz, deine Teurung, deine Wasserfluten, den Gerechten mit dem Bösewicht auffressen?" (67)

[48] "Wir wollen über sie her wie die Sündflut und auf ihre Köpfe herabfeuren wie Wetterleuchten!" (68)

avenger! — you didn't do this, Schweizer."[49] The bandits become the nemesis of nature that avenges its own violation.

Enfeebled by the departure of one son, Moor is locked by the other in the ruins of an old castle nearby, where "the ghosts of my forefathers ... drag rattling chains and murmur their death song at the midnight hour."[50] The displaced old order has been reduced to a ghost of its former self, its sheltering walls broken and exposed to night and the elements, its members dead or enchained on the fringes of a corrupt new order introduced by Franz. Violated and perverted, the old order has been shunted into the deep forests in the dark of night, and it is there that Karl joins forces with it to wreak vengeance on his brother.

Schiller's play can be read as a discussion of historical change. A beneficent but decrepit old order sick unto death is gradually displaced by a corrupt, misguided new order. The historical discontinuity of both brothers is tied to their egoistic behavior. While selfish behavior is hardly new in German literature, here it is specifically associated with defiance of tradition, articulation of individuality, and marketplace relations such as competition and exchange. The egoistic ethic of consequent self-interest at others' expense undermines the traditional corporative ideal of social harmony in a rationally ordered universe defined by birth and station.

This process is portrayed as the nemesis of history: the corruption of the traditional order ultimately turns on itself in a paroxysm of violence and nihilism. The utopian old order is overwhelmed by history, while the bandits, who represent a new non-corporative ethic of egoism, offer little hope for the future. Violent nature imagery in the play articulates the violence of historical change.

There is one hope of propitiating a violated nature and restoring the abused old order: if Karl allows a poor laborer to turn him in to the authorities for reward money. The "eleven living children" this laborer is said to have suggest that some of his children died of poverty. The survival of this laborer's family is in doubt. Karl's sacrifice would guarantee its material integrity. His selflessness would subvert the egoism of the new order and lay the groundwork for restoring the old altruistic order of family intimacy.

---

[49] "O unbegreiflicher Finger der rachekundigen Nemesis! Wars nicht dieser, der mir das Sirenenlied trillerte? - Weihe dies Messer der dunklen Vergelterin! - das hast du nicht getan, Schweizer." (108-109)

[50] "...die Gespenster meiner Väter ... rasselnde Ketten schleifen, und in mitternächtlicher Stunde ihr Totenlied raunen." (115)

However, even this selfless act is open to question. The bandits interpret Karl's desire to turn himself in as vanity, and Karl himself is keenly aware that "one could admire me for it."[51] Moreover, in Schiller's scheme of things money hardly mediates happiness, and the price is a human life. Market-type exchanges of this sort are less a solution in Schiller's play than a tragic indication of the problem: when Karl buys his freedom from his bandit contract with Amalia's life, he sacrifices any hope of ever restoring the Moor legacy of family intimacy. Even the thin hope of recovering the altruistic basis of the old order seems dubious in an age of pervasive egoism, materialism, and market relations.

Schiller paints an unencouraging portrait of an abused old order in danger of total collapse. "Two people like me," Karl ultimately confesses, "[would] destroy the whole edifice of the ethical world."[52] There is another person like Karl in the play, his alter ego Franz. Together, they reduce the old order to shambles. An idealized world of family intimacy in harmony with society is undermined by egoistic aspirations predicated on spreading market relations, a new, vicious social order that promises to turn on and destroy itself. Isolated and endangered on the social periphery, Schiller's characters succumb to the violence of historical change associated with wild nature imagery.

---

[51] "Man könnte mich darum bewundern." (139)

[52] "[Z]wei Menschen wie ich [würden] den ganzen Bau der sittlichen Welt zugrund richten." (138)

6

Nature's Hidden Terror

WHEN PEOPLE EVOKE AN unsullied nature, they usually have a social project or projection in mind. The advertiser uses the term to increase sales. Entrepreneurs see in nature raw materials to be exploited and new jobs to be created. The tourist industry exploits the longing to escape to nature in order to sell vacation packages. Scholars, pundits, and politicians project behavior they deem a priori onto human nature. Even environmentalists appeal to nature in order to gain public backing for programs designed to preserve existing ecosystems. Nature as something discretely other than society or civilization is a concept with a wide range of social, civilizing purposes.

The literary myth of wild nature reveals similar purposes. Whether in the form of antiquity's *locus amoenus* or the Biblical Garden of Eden, idyllic nature imagery projects the social ideals of a given age onto nature itself in utopian contrast to social reality. It is a way of exploring beyond that which exists to discover that which could be. As such, nature imagery can entail ways of conceptualizing and even propagating social change. Conversely, in idealizing and affixing cultural norms as natural and timeless, idyllic nature imagery can function to reinforce and propagate the status quo.

Violent nature imagery is the reverse side of the coin. Where idyllic nature imagery reinforces static values, violent nature destroys their fixed settings, signifying ferment and change. Conversely, where nature's fair horizons offer means of exploring social alternatives, distant storm clouds could signal the danger of doing so. In Biblical myth, for instance, those who explore alternative modes of behavior are punished by natural disasters, which are signs of transgression. Such mythical explanations of natural phenomena validate the behavioral codes upon which they are predicated.

This makes them important indicators of prevailing social codes and the status of their validation. When threatened by structural change, these social codes may be interrogated in contemporary stories rich in violent nature imagery such as floods, storms, and earthquakes. Therefore, it seems appropriate to ask what, if anything, the violent nature imagery featured in Gerstenberg's *Ugolino*, Goethe's *Werther*, and Schiller's *Räuber* says about contemporary developments in late eighteenth-century Germany.

These works were designed to appeal to a new kind of readership no longer bound to the court, but increasingly linked to the market. As absolutist states pursued policies designed to centralize power at the expense of the traditional estates, new non-corporative strata tied in one way or another to the state or a state-subsidized market sector emerged. The most dynamic of these strata was the new bourgeoisie, comprised of bureaucrats, professionals, and entrepreneurs. Since these sectors belonged to no traditional estate, their experience was molded by their isolation on the fringes of traditional corporative society. The new bourgeoisie dominated eighteenth-century literature, using it to explore the possibilities and pitfalls of a changing world.

In the eighteenth century, the traditional image of nature as a metaphysical order of truth in God was ill-suited to the needs of the new bourgeoisie in articulating its practical experience of the everyday world. The Lisbon earthquake stimulated an already ongoing philosophical debate over the nature of reality: was it grounded in metaphysical principles guaranteed by religion, or was it defined by concrete individual experience? In the early eighteenth century, the new bourgeoisie embraced both principles, marshalling empirical evidence to support the doctrine that an infallible God had created the best of possible worlds. The destruction of Lisbon in 1755 shook faith in this philosophy of optimism: instead of demonstrating a best of possible worlds, nature's violence seemed to contradict it. The resulting debate — not least of all because it was largely conducted within the new bourgeoisie — finally discredited the metaphysical basis of philosophical optimism while establishing individual experience as a dominant criterion of reality.

The Lisbon earthquake did not in any meaningful sense cause the transition to an empirical view of nature. Arguments to the contrary hypostatize history and anthropomorphize nature by projecting human conflicts onto nature. What caused the uproar following the Lisbon earthquake was not the disaster itself, but already existing tensions between the empirical orientation of philosophical optimism and its own metaphysical precepts. Sharpened by the earthquake, these tensions emerged in a powerful debate that ultimately shattered optimism's metaphysical basis.

Immanuel Kant offers an influential example. Initially responding to the Lisbon disaster with traditional arguments in defense of divine providence, Kant eventually admitted that such arguments provide no sure knowledge. The argument that God must have made the best world possible because He is perfect flows from tautological necessity, but has no grounds in the real-life world of actual experience. Kant gradually abandoned metaphysical speculation, instead developing a new epistemology based on categories of perception and judgment. Instead of deducing reality from posited axioms, Kant described its formation in the mind. Kant, Voltaire, Rousseau, Herder, and Hamann tied knowledge to human practice, subordinating the age-old reliance on revealed truth to the truth of human experience. Man became the primary measure of reality, whether as subject-creator of the world as Idea or subject/object of its material forces. In this broad sense, empiricism (whether in its skeptical, materialist, or idealist variants) triumphed over traditional metaphysics in the wake of the Lisbon disaster.

The triumph of empiricism in Germany is reflected in the way in which late eighteenth-century authors from Gerstenberg to Schiller insist on remaining true to nature by shunning social convention and instead exploring the complexities of individual experience. While the Lisbon earthquake is scarcely mentioned in late eighteenth-century literature, the debate it stimulated contributed to the aesthetic articulation of experience in terms of nature imagery. In *Dichtung und Wahrheit*, Goethe links demonic nature to his experience of the Lisbon earthquake, which he in turn compares elsewhere to the Revolutions of 1776, 1789, and 1830. The Lisbon earthquake came to symbolize revolutionary change, partly because Goethe himself maintained that it had shattered optimism.

The triumph of empiricism was indeed associated with changes that might be called revolutionary: predicated on the rise of a new bourgeoisie on the margins of corporative society, it led to the exploration of alternatives in nature and society. However, the Lisbon earthquake did not itself demolish optimist philosophy, which persisted for decades afterward. Still, by the time Goethe reflected on it in his autobiography (1814), the revolutionary portent of the Lisbon earthquake was clear, though by no means entirely welcome. It appeared demonic, with an uncontrollable and therefore frightening dynamic of its own. For Goethe, demonic nature melds fearful nature imagery with uncontrollable social forces, articulating ambivalence toward modern change. Goethe was not alone in this view: late eighteenth-century

German literature amply explores changing social realities in connection with a violent nature that appears demonic.

In his play *Ugolino*, Gerstenberg explores his readers' experience of social isolation. Contemporary fascination with Dante's story of a father and sons starving to death in a prison tower is probably due to the story's appeal to its audience's own social situation. The tower provides shelter in the intimate family circle from the menace of public authorities outside, allowing the Gherardescas to explore new social identities. At the same time, their isolation inevitably leads them to consume and destroy each other.

Initially, the individual aspirations of the Gherardescas to freedom, fame, and fortune are idealized in the altruistic context of family intimacy. They dream of harmonious interaction in the past between family members and society at large out in the countryside near Ugolino's villa. Far from the urban seat of central authority, the Gherardescas are free to develop egoistic aspirations to power and property.

In so doing, they challenge traditional instances of authority based on birth and station rather than achievement. Supported by the aristocracy, the prince responds by imprisoning them in the tower, where their competition with one another for glory leads to mutual domination and manipulation. Behind the facade of altruistic family intimacy lurks an egoistic struggle for power.

At the same time, the Gherardescas are not only unable to challenge public authority outside, but unwilling to do so. The storm of conflict outside proves so frightening that the prospect of facing it literally blinds them with fear. They are caught in a double bind: if they venture outside the tower, they are destroyed by the prince's minions, and if they remain inside the tower, they eventually destroy themselves.

Violent nature imagery in the play articulates not only the hopelessness of this situation, but also its hidden terror. Idealistic nature imagery near Ugolino's villa gives way to violent images of nature in the tower as the Gherardescas become martins, lynxes, and wolves that stalk and prey on each other. Their pursuit of individual achievement and acquisition in the private sphere becomes a frighteningly destructive struggle of all against all. Ugolino's attempt to pursue individual aspirations in public unleashes the fearful storm outside, blinding him and his son Francesco with its lightning and reducing them to impotence. The search for alternative identities on the fringes of corporative society leads to a terrifying discourse of violence and destruction in nature.

The association of death and destruction with violent nature in Goethe's *Werther* is equally striking. Frustrated by his inability to possess Lotte, Werther contemplates murdering both her and his rival Albert before ultimately committing suicide. As the conflict sharpens, the idyllic valleys and springs Werther visits give way to storm-swept cliffs overlooking raging torrents below.

The story of unrequited passion is incidental to the novel's focus, which, as the title indicates, is Werther's suffering. In his preface, the novel's editor invites the reader to identify with Werther's sufferings, and the novel's immense popularity suggests that many readers did so. From the outset, Werther isolates himself from others not by choice, but due to his ineluctable sense of individual integrity. Shunning the conflicts he criticizes among the estates and between competing individuals, he seeks the solitude of nature, finding sustenance in idyllic nature scenery at his falling brook, at the spring, and in Wahlheim.

His favorite nature spots articulate a social ideal: they resolve the unsettling social conflicts in the urban milieu by integrating the individual into home, family, and community under a wise and benevolent patriarchal authority. Despite sharp criticism of the aristocracy, Werther acknowledges the authority of the prince (Count von C.), and he expressly affirms the necessity of social stratification due to the privileges it affords him. However, he would reform absolutism to give it a human face: privilege and authority would acquire legitimacy through empathy and altruism rather than birth and station. As surrogate mother of her siblings, Lotte represents this patriarchal ideal. In the sylvan setting of the hunting lodge not far from Werther's favorite spots in nature, she integrates home, family, and community under a benevolent parental authority.

The problem with this vision is that it contradicts its own basis in the domination of an ascendant new bourgeoisie. Behind Werther's rhetoric of empathy and altruism is the discourse of manipulative egoism that informs his letters. Secure in the knowledge of social privilege and personal superiority, Werther ruthlessly exploits those around him, suppressing their individuality by transforming them into mirrors of himself. Lotte is no exception. As the vehicle of his patriarchal ideal, she becomes an object of acquisition for which he must compete with her husband. This poses an insoluble problem: driven by his own sense of identity to acquire the natural treasure Lotte, Werther finds himself confronted with the very conflicts he escapes from into nature to begin with, particularly the competitive struggle of all against all under incipient capitalism. Acquiring Lotte would destroy what she stands for, the patriarchal ideal of social harmony built around the nucleus of home and family.

The hopelessness of this situation is signified by the transformation in the novel of idyllic into violent nature imagery. Citing Alexander Pope and Klopstock respectively, Werther and Lotte envision a timeless corporative harmony in idyllic nature at the falling brook and after the storm. This vision is undermined by Werther's own discourse of individual identity on the fringes of corporative society, which transforms nature from a scene of eternal life into an eternally consuming monster. The emergence of demonic nature signals the displacement of harmonious corporative hierarchies by a violent struggle among isolated individuals and competing interests in a new and frightening social order.

Schiller's *Räuber* can also be read as an articulation of horror at changing social relations. From its very first lines, the play identifies Count von Moor with a traditional order in decline. Moor's palace in the Franconian countryside is associated with idyllic nature imagery in a Golden Age of harmonious family intimacy. Moor benevolently governs an orderly corporative hierarchy in service to the state. Karl aspires to this lost corporative ideal of family intimacy in harmony with nature and society.

Franz corrupts the rural order by refusing to accept his subordinate status as next-born. In pursuit of individual ambition, he emancipates himself from the traditional strictures of birth and station. Unable to resist his machinations, the old order collapses. Moor finds refuge in the castle ruins of his forefathers, and Franz usurps authority, imposing his tyrannical rule.

Unable to return home, Karl turns to banditry in order to punish those who corrupt the corporative ideal. However, Karl's banditry undermines and ultimately destroys its own premises. Associated with the night, dark forests, and violent nature imagery such as storms, the bandits embrace the very egoism, tyranny, and entrepreneurial spirit that Karl would punish. The search for alternative identities on the periphery of traditional society results in a paroxysm of self-destruction represented as violent nature in the vengefully destructive course of history (what Karl calls its nemesis).

Nature imagery in the play represents a historical transition from harmonious corporative hierarchy (the idyllic past) to the struggle of all against all under incipient capitalism (the violent present). The rise of non-corporative social sectors and identities on the periphery of traditional society appears frightening and destructive, while the good old days of corporative hierarchy are idealized. Violent nature imagery in the play — the nemesis of historical change — threatens the whole ethical order by replacing what the author calls truth with changing social realities.

Gerstenberg's *Ugolino*, Goethe's *Werther*, and Schiller's *Räuber* all articulate a conflict between new identities and old values. All feature traditional nature idylls implying a utopian social harmony. While each utopia is built around the nuclear family rather than the estate, each is designed to reform rather than challenge a traditional vision of harmonious hierarchy, preserving and even enhancing corporative privilege and authority by renewing their legitimacy. Individual aspirations in conflict with these values, particularly in the characters of Anselmo, Werther, and Franz, violate and demolish the vision of harmony in each work. These ruinous aspirations derive from the inexorable search for individual identity on the fringes of traditional society. In each work, patriarchal ideals of altruistic harmony in family and society are destroyed by an all-consuming struggle of all against all, transforming nature from peaceful consonance into a self-devouring demon.

Such representations of violent nature suggest a closer affinity than sometimes thought between the Sturm und Drang and the emerging ideology of German conservatism articulated by Justus Möser, with its basis in an idealized harmony among estates in small and medium-sized towns. The seamy underside of modern capitalist society — its uncertainty, alienation, and brutal marketplace logic — emerges in late eighteenth-century writings in the fearful form of wild or violent nature imagery. As the principal characters in each work pursue a sense of individual identity in nature, they undermine the traditional ideals they aspire to. Despite their bold articulation of individual emancipation, they display a hidden fear of corresponding processes of modern change and a secret yearning for the security of lost corporative ties.

It would be wrong to suggest that these works reject modern change outright. All three writers challenged the legitimacy of corporative hierarchies, espousing individual liberty and criticizing the authority of the tyrants and the archaic social structures portrayed in their early works. They undermined traditional literary conventions by appealing to the truth of individual experience in the name of nature. Such subversive or emancipatory moments characterize what Georg Lukács calls the "bourgeois-revolutionary humanism" in works such as Goethe's *Werther*.

Nevertheless, the role of Gerstenberg, Goethe, and Schiller as authors was to condense not only the hopes, but also the fears of contemporary audiences into a literary discussion of contemporary experience. The complexity of their works defies reduction to a single ideological theme. This study suggests that key late eighteenth-century works express not only a powerful emancipatory impulse, but also an acute fear of the consequences of modern change. The same works that challenge the corporative status quo and anticipate individual emancipation convey a hapless fear of the very forces of modernity they propagate. Instead of visionary champions of human progress, Gerstenberg, Goethe, and Schiller are ambivalent figures caught between enthusiasm for the new order and doubts about its consequences, with a nostalgic predilection for the good old days of corporative stability. Their expression of modernity carries its own negation.

Works Consulted

Adorno, Theodor and Max Horkheimer. *Dialektik der Aufklärung. Philosophische Fragmente*. 1944; rpt. Amsterdam: Querido, 1947.

Alighieri, Dante. "Inferno, 33. Gesang." Trans. J. N. Meinhard. In *Heinrich Wilhelm von Gerstenberg, Ugolino*. Ed. Christoph Siegrist. Stuttgart: Reclam, 1966.

Ames, Carol. "Competition, Class and Structure in *Die Leiden des jungen Werther*." *German Quarterly* 50 (1977), 138-149.

Arnim, Bettina von. Letter to Goethe. 24 November 1810. *Goethes Briefwechsel mit einem Kinde*. Ed. Gustav Konrad. Cologne: Bartmann, 1960.

Assling, Reinhard. *Werthers Leiden. Die ästhetische Rebellion der Innerlichkeit*. Frankfurt, Bern: Lang, 1981.

Barraclough, Geoffrey. *The Origins of Modern Germany*. London: W.W. Norton & Co., 1984.

Bestermann, Theodore. "Voltaire et le désastre de Lisbonne." *Studies in Voltaire and the Eighteenth Century* 2 (1956), 7-24.

Blumenberg, Hans. *Work on Myth*. Trans. Robert M. Wallace. Cambridge, Massachusetts and London: MIT Press, 1985.

Böschenstein-Schäfer, Renate. *Idylle*. Sammlung Metzler, 63. Stuttgart: Metzler, 1977.

Bohm, Arnd. "Possessive Individualism in Schiller's *Die Räuber*." *Mosaic* 20 (1987) 1, 31-42.

Bolten, Jürgen. "Zur Genese des bürgerlichen Selbstverständnisses im ausgehenden 18. Jahrhundert. Schillers Frühdramen als Beispiel." *Germanistik-Forschungsstand und Perspektiven*. Ed. Georg Stötzel. Berlin, New York: Walter de Gruyter, 1985, Volume 2, 492-504.

Borchmeyer, Dieter. "Die Tragödie vom verlorenen Vater. Der Dramatiker Schiller und die Aufklärung - Das Beispiel der 'Räuber.'" In *Friedrich Schiller. Angebot und Diskurs*. Ed. Helmut Brandt. Berlin, Weimar: Aufbau-Verlag, 1987, 160-184.

Brauner, Sigrid. "Frightened Shrews and Fearless Wives: The Concept of the Witch in Early Modern German Texts." Dissertation University of California at Berkeley, 1989.

Works Consulted

Bruford, W. H. *Germany in the Eighteenth Century. Social Background of the Literary Revival.* 1935; rpt. Cambridge: UP, 1971.

Brunschwig, Henri. *Enlightenment and Romanticism in Eighteenth-Century Prussia.* Trans. Frank Jellinek. Chicago: University of Chicago Press, 1974.

Buhr, Gerhard. "Die Leiden des jungen Werthers und der Roman des Sturm und Drang." *Handbuch des deutschen Romans.* Ed. Helmut Koopman. Düsseldorf: Bagel, 1983.

Charlton, D. G. *New Images of the Natural in France.* Cambridge: Cambridge UP, 1984.

Clarke, Mary and Clement Crisp. *The History of Dance.* New York: Crown Publishers, 1981.

Cornell, James. *The Great International Disaster Book.* New York: Charles Scribner's Sons, 1976.

Crusius, Christian August. *Entwurf der nothwendigen Vernunft-Wahrheiten.* 1745; rpt. Hildesheim: Georg Olms, 1964.

Davidsohn, Robert. *Geschichte von Florenz.* Berlin: E. Siegfried Mittler, 1908, Volume 2, Part 2.

Davison, Charles. *Great Earthquakes.* London: Thomas Murphy & Co., 1936.

De Vries, Jan. *The Economy of Europe in an Age of Crisis, 1600-1750.* London, New York, New Rochelle, Melbourne, Sydney: Cambridge UP, 1976.

Elias, Norbert. *The History of Manners.* Volume 1 of *The Civilizing Process.* Trans. Edmund Jephcott. New York: Pantheon Books, 1978.

Flaschka, Horst. *Goethes Werther.* Munich: Fink, 1987.

Gerstenberg, Heinrich Wilhelm von. *Briefe über Merkwürdigkeiten der Literatur.* In *Heinrich Wilhelm von Gerstenberg, Ugolino.* Ed. Christoph Siegrist. Stuttgart: Reclam, 1966.

———. *Ugolino.* Ed. Christoph Siegrist. Stuttgart: Reclam, 1966.

Glacken, Clarence J. *Traces on the Rhodian Shore. Nature and Culture in Western Thought from Ancient Times to the End of the Eighteenth Century.* Berkeley: U of California P, 1967.

Goethe, Johann Wolfgang. *Dichtung und Wahrheit. Aus meinem Leben. Goethes Werke.* Ed. Erich Trunz. Hamburg: Wegner, 1955; rpt. Munich: Beck, 1981, Volumes 9-10.

———. *Die Leiden des jungen Werther. Goethes Werke.* Ed. Erich Trunz. Hamburg: Christian Wegner Verlag, 1955; rpt. München: Beck, 1981, Volume 6.

Grathoff, Dirk. "Der Pflug, die Nußbäume und der Bauerbursche: Natur im thematischen Gefüge des Werther-Romans." *Goethe. Vorträge aus Anlaß seines 150. Todestages.* Ed. Thomas Clasen and Erwin Liebfried. Frankfurt, Bern, New York: Lang, 1984, 55-75.

Grimminger, Rolf. "Aufklärung, Absolutismus und bürgerliche Individuen." *Hansers Sozialgeschichte der deutschen Literatur.* Ed. Rolf Grimminger. Munich: Hanser, 1980, Volume 3, 15-99.

Großklaus, Götz and Ernst Oldemeyer, eds. *Natur als Gegenwelt. Beiträge zur Kulturgeschichte der Natur.* Karlsruhe: von Loeper, 1983.

Guthke, Karl S. "Räuber Moors Glück und Ende." In his *Wege zur Literatur. Studien zur deutschen Dichtungs- und Geistesgeschichte.* Bern, Munich: Francke, 1967, 63-71.

Habermas, Jürgen. *Stukturwandel der Öffentlichkeit. Untersuchungen zu einer Kategorie der bürgerlichen Gesellschaft.* Neuwied: Luchterhand, 1965.

Hamann, Johann Georg. *Johann Georg Hamann: Briefwechsel.* Ed. Walther Ziesemer and Arthur Henkel. Wiesbaden: Insel, 1955, Volume 1.

Hampson, Norman. *A Cultural History of the Enlightenment.* New York: Pantheon Books, 1968.

Hauser, Arnold. *Sozialgeschichte der Kunst und Literatur.* Munich: Beck, 1953.

Havens, George R. "The Conclusion of Voltaire's 'Poème sur le désastre de Lisbonne.'" *Modern Language Notes* 56 (1941) 6, 422-426.

Hazard, Paul. "Le problème du mal dans la conscience européenne du XVIIIe siècle." *Romanic Review* 32 (1941), 147-170.

Herder, Johann Gottfried. *Ideen zur Philosophie der Geschichte der Menschheit. Herders Sämmtliche Werke.* Ed. Bernhard Suphan. Berlin: Weidmannsche Buchhandlung, 1887, Volume 13.

———. "Ugolino." *Allgemeine deutsche Bibliothek* 11 (1770). *Heinrich Wilhelm von Gerstenberg, Ugolino.* Ed. Christoph Siegrist. Stuttgart: Reclam, 1966.

Herrmann, Hans-Peter. "Landschaft in Goethes 'Werther.' Zum Brief vom 18. August." *Goethe. Vorträge aus Anlaß seines 150. Todestages.* Ed. Thomas Clasen and Erwin Leibfried. Frankfurt, Bern, New York: Lang, 1984, 77-100.

Hohendahl, Peter Uwe. "Bürgerlichkeit und Bürgertum als Problem der Literatursoziologie." *German Quarterly* 61 (1988), 264-283.

Hübner, Klaus. *Alltag im literarischen Werk. Eine literatursoziologische Studie zu Goethes Werther.* Heidelberg: Groos, 1982.

Jacobs, Montague. *Gerstenbergs Ugolino. Berliner Beiträge zur Germanischen und Romanischen Philologie* 14 (1898) 7.

Jäger, Georg. *Die Leiden des alten und neuen Werther.* Munich, Vienna: Hanser, 1984.

Jäger, Hans-Wolf. "Das Naturbild als politische Metapher im Vormärz." In *Zur Literatur der Restaurationsepoche.* Ed. Jost Hermand and Manfred Windfuhr. Stuttgart: Metzler, 1970, 405-440.

Jonnes, Denis. "Pattern of Power. Family and State in Schiller's Early Drama." *Colloquia Germanica* 20 (1987) 2/3, 138-161.

Kaiser, Gerhard. *Pietismus und Patriotismus im literarischen Deutschland. Ein Beitrag zum Problem der Säkularisation.* Frankfurt: Athenäum, 1973.

Kant, Immanuel. *Der einzige Beweisgrund einer Demonstration des Daseins Gottes. Immanuel Kant, Werke.* Ed. Wilhelm Weischedel. Frankfurt: Suhrkamp, 1968, Volume 2, Part 2.

------. "Fortgesetzte Betrachtung der seit einiger Zeit wahrgenommenen Erderschütterungen." *Königsberger Wöchentliche Frage- und Anzeigungs-Nachrichten,* April 1756; rpt. *Immanuel Kants Sämmtliche Werke.* Ed. G. Hartenstein. Leipzig: Voss, 1867, Volume 1, 447-456.

------. *Geschichte und Naturbeschreibung des Erdbebens am Ende des Jahres 1755.* Königsberg: Hartung, 1758; rpt. *Immanuel Kants Sämmtliche Werke.* Ed. G. Hartenstein. Leipzig: Voss, 1867, Volume 1, 412-444.

------. *Träume eines Geistersehers. Immanuel Kant, Werke.* Ed. Wilhelm Weischedel. Frankfurt: Suhrkamp, 1968, Volume 2, Part 2.

------. *Versuch einiger Betrachtungen über den Optimismus. Immanuel Kant, Werke.* Ed. Wilhelm Weischedel. Frankfurt: Suhrkamp, 1968, Volume 2, Part 2.

------. "Von den Ursachen der Erderschütterungen, bei Gelegenheit des Unglücks, welches die westlichen Länder von Europa gegen das Ende des vorigen Jahres betroffen hat." *Königsberger Wöchentliche Frage- und Anzeigungs-Nachrichten,* 24 and 31 January 1756; rpt. *Immanuel Kants Sämmtliche Werke.* Ed. G. Hartenstein. Leipzig: Voss, 1867, Volume 1, 401-411.

Kemmerer, Arthur. "Das Erdbeben von Lissabon in seiner Beziehung zum Problem des Übels in der Welt." Dissertation Frankfurt 1958.

Kendrick, T. D. *The Lisbon Earthquake.* London: Methuen & Co. LTD, 1956.

Koc, Richard. "Fathers and Sons. Ambivalence Doubled in Schiller's *Räuber.*" *The Germanic Review* 61 (1986), 91-104.

Leigh, R. A. "From the 'Inégalité' to 'Candide:' Notes on a Desultory Dialogue between Rousseau and Voltaire (1755-1759)." *The Age of Enlightenment*. Ed. W. H. Barber et al. Edinburgh, London: Oliver & Boyd, 1967, 66-92.

Leibniz, Georg Wilhelm von. *Die Theodizee*. Trans. Artur Buchenau. Leipzig: Felix Meiner, 1925.

Lessing, Gotthold Ephraim and Moses Mendelssohn. *Pope ein Metaphysiker! G. E. Lessing, Gesammelte Werke*. Berlin: Aufbau-Verlag, 1956, Volume 7.

Lovejoy, Arthur O. *The Great Chain of Being*. Cambridge: Harvard UP, 1953.

———. *Essays in the History of Ideas*. Baltimore: Johns Hopkins Press, 1948, 69-77.

Lütgert, Wilhelm. *Die Erschütterung des Optimismus durch das Erdbeben in Lissabon*. Gütersloh: Berthelsmann, 1928.

Lukács, Georg. "Die Leiden des jungen Werther." In *Johann Wolfgang Goethe, Die Leiden des jungen Werther*. Frankfurt: Insel, 1974, 181-206.

———. *Die Theorie des Romans*. Berlin: Cassirer, 1920; rpt. Darmstadt, Neuwied: Luchterhand, 1979.

Mandelkow, Karl Robert. "Der deutsche Briefroman." *Neophilologus* 44, 1960, 200-208.

Martens, Wolfgang. *Die Botschaft der Tugend. Die Aufklärung im Spiegel der deutschen moralischen Wochenschriften*. Stuttgart: Metzler, 1968.

Martin, Günther. "Werthers problematische Natur." *Neue deutsche Hefte* 29 (1982), 725-735.

Mattenklott, Gert. "Briefroman." *Deutsche Literatur. Eine Sozialgeschichte*. Ed. Ralph-Rainer Wuthenow. Reinbek: Rowohlt, 1980, 185-203.

———. *Melancholie in der Dramatik des Sturm und Drang*. Stuttgart: Metzler, 1968.

———. "Schiller's *Räuber* in der Frühgeschichte des Anarchismus." *Text & Kontext* 9 (1981) 2, 300-314.

McGrane, Bernard. *Beyond Anthropology. Society and the Other*. New York: Columbia UP, 1989.

McKendrick, Neil. "The End of Optimism." *Horizon* 16 (1974) 2, 45-47.

Mecklenburg, Norbert, ed. *Naturlyrik und Gesellschaft*. Stuttgart: Klett-Cotta, 1977.

Moeller, Horst. *Fürstenstaat oder Bürgernation? Deutschland 1763-1815*. Berlin: Siedler Verlag, 1989.

Mog, Paul. *Ratio und Gefühlskultur. Studien zur Psychogenese von Literatur.* Tübingen: Niemeyer, 1976.

Moore, Cecil A. "Did Leibniz influence Pope's Essay?" *The Journal of English and Germanic Philology* 16 (1917), 84-102.

Moser, Friedrich Carl von. "Lissabon. 1755." Friedrich Carl von Moser, *Moralische und politische Schriften.* Frankfurt: Gebhard, 1763, Volume 1, 179-188.

Mottek, Hans. *Wirtschaftsgeschichte Deutschlands.* Berlin: VEB Deutscher Verlag der Wissenschaften, 1973.

Müller, Peter. "Angriff auf die humanistische Tradition." *Weimarer Beiträge* 19 (1973) 1, 109-127, and 3, 92-109.

Pascal, Roy. *The German Sturm und Drang.* Manchester: Manchester UP, 1953.

Pope, Alexander. *Essay on Man.* Ed. A. Hamilton Thompson. Cambridge: Cambridge UP, 1913.

Das Räuberbuch. Frankfurt: Verlag Roter Stern, 1974.

Reinhardt, O. and D. R. Oldroyd. "Kant's Theory of Earthquakes and Volcanic Action." *Annals of Science* 40 (1983) 3, 247-269.

Renner, Karl N. "'...laß das Büchlein deinen Freund seyn.' Goethes Roman *Die Leiden des jungen Werthers* und die Diätetik der Aufklärung." *Zur Sozialgeschichte der deutschen Literatur von der Aufklärung bis zur Jahrhundertwende.* Ed. Günter Häntzschel, John Ormred, and Karl N. Renner. Tübingen: Niemeyer, 1985, 1-20.

Ritter, Joachim. "Landschaft. Zur Funktion des Ästhetischen in der modernen Gesellschaft." In his *Subjektivität. 6 Aufsätze.* Frankfurt: Suhrkamp, 1974, 141-163.

Rohrer, Berthold. "Das Erdbeben von Lissabon in der französischen Literatur des 18. Jahrhunderts." Dissertation Heidelberg 1933.

Rousseau, Jean-Jacques. "Discourse on the Origins and Foundations of Inequality." Trans. Roger D. and Judith R. Masters. *Rousseau, The First and Second Discourses.* New York: St. Martin's Press, 1964.

Rousseau, Jean-Jacques. "Letter to Voltaire on Providence." *Rousseau: Religious Writings.* Ed. Ronald Grimsley. Oxford: Clarendon Press, 1970.

Sauder, Gerhard. *Empfindsamkeit.* Volume 1: *Voraussetzungen und Elemente.* Stuttgart: Metzler, 1974.

Scherpe, Klaus. "Friedrich Schiller. *Die Räuber.*" In *Dramen des Sturm und Drang.* Stuttgart: Reclam, 1987, 161-211.

———. *Werther und Wertherwirkung*. Wiesbaden: Athenaion, 1969.

Schiller, Friedrich. *Die Räuber*. Stuttgart: Reclam, 1969.

Schings, Hans-Jürgen. "Schillers 'Räuber:' Ein Experiment des Universalhasses." In *Friedrich Schiller. Kunst, Humanität und Politik in der späten Aufklärung*. Ed. Wolfgang Wittkowski. Tübingen: Max Niemeyer Verlag, 1982, 1-25.

Schlunk, Jürgen E. "Vertrauen als Ursache und Überwindung tragischer Verstrickung in Schillers 'Räubern.' Zum Verständnis Karl Moors." *Jahrbuch der deutschen Schillergesellschaft* 27 (1983), 185-201.

Schmidt, Henry J. "The Language of Confinement in Gerstenberg's *Ugolino* and Klinger's *Sturm und Drang*." *Lessing Yearbook* 11 (1979), 165-197.

Seeba, Hinrich C. "Historiographischer Idealismus? Fragen zu Schillers Geschichtsbild." In *Friedrich Schiller. Kunst, Humanität und Politik in der späten Aufklärung*. Ed. Wolfgang Wittkowski. Tübingen: Max Niemeyer Verlag, 1982, 229-251.

Seligo, Hans. "Das große Erdbeben." *Merian* 12 (1959) 8, 33-35.

Sørensen, Bengt A. *Herrschaft und Zärtlichkeit. Der Patriarchalismus und das Drama im 18. Jahrhundert*. Munich: Beck, 1984.

Spaemann, Robert. "Genetisches zum Naturbegriff des 18. Jahrhunderts." *Archiv für Begriffsgeschichte* 11 (1967), 59-74.

Stein, Gerd. "Genialität als Resignation bei Gerstenberg." *Literatur der bürgerlichen Emanzipation im 18. Jahrhundert*. Ed. Gert Mattenklott and Klaus Scherpe. Kronberg/Ts: Scriptor, 1973, 105-110.

Uz, Johann P. *Sämtliche poetische Werke von J. P. Uz*. Ed. A. Sauer. 1890; rpt. Stuttgart: Nendeln/Liechtenstein, 1968.

Valjavec, Fritz. *Die Entstehung der politischen Strömungen in Deutschland. 1770-1815*. Kronberg: Athenaeum; Düsseldorf: Droste, 1978.

Vereker, Charles. *Eighteenth-Century Optimism. Interrelations between Moral and Social Theory*. Liverpool: Liverpool UP, 1967.

Viner, Jacob. *The Role of Providence in the Social Order*. Princeton: Princeton UP, 1972.

Voltaire. *Candide. The Works of Voltaire*. Trans. William F. Fleming. New York: E. R. DuMont, 1901, Volume 1.

———. "The Lisbon Earthquake." *The Works of Voltaire*. Trans. William F. Fleming. New York: E. R. DuMont, 1901, Volume 10, Part 2.

Waldeck, Peter B. "Friedrich Schiller: *Die Räuber*." In his *The Split Self from Goethe to Broch*. London: Associated UPes, 1979, 78-98.

Walker, Mack. *German Home Towns*. Ithaca: Cornell UP, 1971.

Weinrich, Harald. "Literaturgeschichte eines Weltereignisses: das Erdbeben in Lissabon." *Literatur für Leser*. Ed. Harald Weinrich. Stuttgart, Berlin, Cologne, Mainz: Kohlhammer, 1971, 64-76.

——. "Voltaire, Hiob und das Erdbeben von Lissabon." *Aufsätze zur portugiesischen Kulturgeschichte* 4 (1964), 96-104.

White, Hayden. "The Forms of Wildness. Archaeology of an Idea." In *Tropics of Discourse*. Baltimore: Johns Hopkins UP, 1978, 150-182.

Willey, Basil. *The Eighteenth-Century Background. Studies on the Idea of Nature in the Thought of the Period*. London, 1940; rpt. Boston: Beacon, 1961.

Williams, Raymond. *The Country and the City*. New York: Oxford UP, 1973.

Wittkowski, Wolfgang. "Selbstinszenierung und Authentizität des Ich in Schillers Dramen." *Das neuzeitliche Ich in der Literatur des 18. und 20. Jahrhunderts*. Ed. Ulrich Fülleborn and Manfred Engel. Munich: Wilhelm Fink Verlag, 1988, 109-129.

Woloch, Isser. *Eighteenth-Century Europe. Tradition and Progress*. New York, London: W.W. Norton & Co., 1982.

Zimmermann, Jörg, ed. *Das Naturbild des Menschen*. Munich: Fink, 1982.

Zons, Raimar Stefan. "Ein Riß durch die Ewigkeit. Landschaft in 'Werther' und 'Lenz.'" *Literatur für Leser* (1981), 65-78.

Index

American Revolution 18, 132

Barraclough, Geoffrey 11, 12, 17
Bayle, Pierre 40
Bible 1-2, 130
  Genesis 2, 28, 49, 88
  Job 39, 70-71
  Jonah 36
  Rebeccah 88
Blumenberg, Hans 3, 4
Brabant Uprising 18
Brockes, Barthold Heinrich 27
Burke, Edmund 7

Counter Reformation 17
Crusius, Chistian August 33, 47
Cusa, Cardinal Nicholas von 30

Dalberg, Wolfgang Heribert von 108
Dante Alighieri 56, 62, 70, 133
De Vries, Jan 10-12

Elias, Norbert 4
Enlightenment 19-21

Fascism 3
Francken, Joachim 24
Frederick I (Barbarossa) 111
Frederick II 11, 14, 21, 46, 111
French Revolution 8, 9, 18, 132

Gerstenberg, Heinrich Wilhelm von 56, 62, 72, 132, 136
  Ugolino 9, 21, 57-72, 107, 131, 133
Gherardesca, Count Ugolino 58
Gleim, Johann Wilhelm Ludwig 16
Goethe, Johann Wolfgang 7-9, 23, 27, 42, 45, 73-77, 134-135

Dichtung und Wahrheit 75, 132
Egmont 18
Die Leiden des jungen Werther 9, 21, 73-107, 131, 134-135
"Der Zauberlehrling" 8
Goeze, Melchior 73
Gottsched, Johann Christoph 23, 34
Grimminger, Rolf 14, 15, 18-19
Großklaus, Götz 5-8
Gryphius, Andreas 4-5, 21

Habermas, Jürgen 14, 16
Haller, Albrecht 6, 21
Hamann, Johann Georg 34, 49, 53, 132
Hampson, Norman 18
Hauser, Arnold 16
Herder, Johann Gottfried 34, 50-53, 54, 57, 132
  Ideen zur Philosophie der Geschichte der Menschheit 50-53
Holbach, Dietrich Freiherr von 5
Hume, David 33, 49

Kant, Immanuel 5, 24, 34, 37-38, 45-54, 132
  Der einzige Beweisgrund einer Demonstration des Daseins Gottes 47-48, 50
  Träume eines Geistersehers 48, 50, 54
  "Geschichte und Naturbeschreibung des Erdbebens" 37-38, 45-47, 48
  Versuch einiger Betrachtungen über den Optimismus 47, 48, 49
Kendrick, T. D. 35
Klopstock, Friedrich Gottlieb 24, 36, 85, 101, 135

Leibniz, Georg Wilhelm von 28, 30, 34, 47
Lepenies, Walter 10
Lessing, Gotthold Ephraim 16, 20, 73
Lisbon earthquake 1, 8, 23-27, 30, 34-39, 42-46, 49, 50, 53-55, 131-132
Löffler, Tobias 113
Loma Prieta earthquake 1
Lukács, Georg 74-75, 136
Luther, Martin 105

Malagrida, Gabriel 1, 35
Maupertuis, Pierre-Louis Moreau de 34, 47
Mendelssohn, Moses 34
Merck, Johann Heinrich 73
Möser, Justus 9, 13, 136
Moral Weeklies 28-30, 32, 54
Moser, Friedrich Carl von 23

Napoleon Bonaparte 73
Nicolai, Christoph Friedrich 20, 73, 117

Optimism 27, 28, 30, 31-34, 37, 38, 41-55, 131-132

Piderit, Johann Rudolph Anton 24, 36
Pope, Alexander 6, 3-33, 34, 36, 42, 43, 47, 51, 52, 85, 135
  Essay on Man 6, 31-33, 35-36, 38, 48, 47, 52, 54, 85
Rebhuhn, Paul 105
Reformation 17
Reinhard, Adolph Friedrich von 34, 47
Richardson, Samuel 75
Rousseau, Jean-Jacques 5, 34, 42-45, 49, 53, 132
  Discours sur l'origine de l'inégalité 42-43, 45
  Letter to Voltaire 43-45, 49

Schiller, Friedrich 5, 21
  Die Räuber 9, 21, 107, 108-129, 131, 135-136
Schnabel, Johann Gottfried 27
Schwerin, Kurt Christoph von 108
Seven Years' War 21, 46, 54, 108
Sørensen, Bengt A. 89
Spaemann, Robert 5
Sturm und Drang 9, 107, 136

Thirty Years' War 10, 11, 13, 17
Treaty of Westphalia 11

Ubaldini, Archbishop Ruggiero 58
Uz, Johann Peter 36-37, 41

Voltaire 1, 34, 38-42, 47, 49, 50, 53, 132
  Candide 1, 42, 48, 49
  "Poème sur le désastre de Lisbonne" 35-36, 38, 39-42, 43, 46

Walker, Mack 13
Weymann, Daniel 47
White, Hayden 2, 4
Wichmannshausen, Rudolph Friedrich von 24
Willey, Basil 85
Williams, Raymond 3
Wolff, Christian 48
Woloch, Isser 11